*I*NTIMATE THINGS

by
Laylage Courie

with
SELECT LITERARY PAIRINGS
curated by Lazuli Literary Group

Lazuli Reading Series
A Curated Reading Experience

Each Lazuli Reading Series book pairs one contemporary work with carefully curated pieces of classic literature that enhance the flavor, texture, and emotional resonance of the feature work; the aim is to offer an alternative to the prevailing convention that non-fiction scholarly texts are the only worthy appendices to a work of poetry or fiction.

LAZULI READING SERIES
Published by Lazuli Literary Group

First published in 2024
Copyright 2024 by Lazuli Literary Group
Brooklyn, New York

ISBN: 978-0-9994243-6-0

With scene headings from Betty Radice's translation of *The Letters of Abelard & Heloise* (Penguin Classic Edition, 2004; revised by Michael Clanchy).

Abelard's parables extracted from his treatise *Sic et Non* as translated on the public domain bibliofile site.

An early version of Act I was first presented in 2008 as "Intimate Things" at the Looking Glass Theater, W. 57th Street, New York, New York under the direction of Toby Bercovici, featuring Megan Gaffney and Meghan Bean.

Gratitude is also due to these artists who exercised various pieces of the text in front of audiences: Grant Neale, Hillary Spector, & Chris Oden with Nomad Theater, Jill Samuels with Vancouver's Boca del Lupo, and the Lower Manhattan Cultural Council's Uptown/Downtown project. Gratitude also to Chris Speed and *Yeah NO* for their 2004 album, *Swell Henry*.

"Drifting through the reflection of real ruins / On a lake constructed by an architect" first appeared in *Wild Roof Journal*, Issue 4.

Table of Contents

i. A Note from Lazuli Literary Group

1 Intimate Things by Laylage Courie

51 Literary Pairings

> 52 | "No worst, there is none. Pitched past
> pitch of grief"
> *Gerard Manley Hopkins*

> 53 | "Sonnet 12: When I do count the clock
> that tells the time"
> *William Shakespeare*

> 54 | "Elegy"
> *Chidiock Tichborne*

> 55 | "Batter my heart, three-person'd God"
> *John Donne*

> 56 | "The Definition of Love"
> *Andrew Marvell*

> 58 | "Drifting through the reflection of real ruins
> On a lake constructed by an architect"
> *Laylage Courie*

59 | "I killed a man"
Laylage Courie

60 | selections from *Carlos Among the Candles*
Wallace Stevens

65 | "Eloisa to Abelard"
Alexander Pope

77 | "Abelard to Eloisa"
Judith Madan

83 | "Love Armed"
Aphra Behn

84 | "Verses design'd by Mrs. A. Behn to be sent to a fair Lady, that desir'd she would absent herself to cure her Love. Left unfinish'd."
Aphra Behn

85 | "On the Author of that Excellent Book Intituled The Way to Health, Long Life, and Happiness"
Aphra Behn

88 | selections from *Salomé*
Oscar Wilde

110 | "The Body of the Father Christian Rosencrux"
William Butler Yeats

112 | "William Blake and the Imagination"
William Butler Yeats

115	ENDNOTES
119	ABOUT THE AUTHOR
120	A PLACE TO RECORD THOUGHTS

A Note
from Lazuli Literary Group

Welcome, reader, to the debut offering in our Lazuli Reading Series. Each book features a new contemporary work by a Lazuli author paired with a curated selection of readings that enhances the flavor, texture, and emotional resonance of the feature work. Here, our featured work is Laylage Courie's genre-transcendent *Intimate Things*—at once a work of poetry, drama, critical essay, historical fiction, and epistolary narrative—that re-imagines the real-life 12th century romance of Héloïse d'Argenteuil (an abbess and a scholar) and Peter Abelard (a monk and a teacher of philosophy). Their forbidden love affair, with all its tragic trappings, has seen many literary incarnations through the years; Courie's experimental piece plays upon their written correspondence during their separation and the social commentary that the famed romance later engendered.

The literary pairings found in the book's latter half are meant to enrich our appreciation of the literary flavors inherent in *Intimate Things*; to create a novel juxtaposition that places *Intimate Things* in stark relief, allowing us to make new discoveries and see the featured work in a different light. You may liken this curated reading experience to a dessert-wine pairing in that the function of the accompanying works is to prepare the reader's palate to appreciate the subtler literary flavor notes of the contemporary work. The pairings are not *needed* to buttress *Intimate Things*—there is nothing in it that is incomplete—but rather to bring to the surface what is already there.

We recommend reading the featured work fresh, then perusing the accompanying works, then *re-reading* the featured work. As the shifting of a sunbeam through a window splashes light into new corners, your perception of the second reading should *feel* different in this evolving glow.

Some of the selected works very obviously correlate with the historical legend: Alexander Pope's verse epistle "Eloisa to Abelard" (1717) and Judith Cowper Madan's response to Pope, entitled "Abelard to Eloisa" (written in 1720, published in 1728), are two such pieces. Others may seem to have an inexplicable, intuitive, even oblique relationship to the romance or the history, perhaps emphasizing or contrasting with the tone of *Intimate Things*. In other cases, the selections may simply create an atmospheric mist that, once entered, prepares the mind for the poetic style of the feature work. The selective process, at times, was driven by the way these pieces provoke a breathless flash, an emotional call and response. While the typical literary anthology provides accompanying scholarly works and criticism that dissect the feature work after it is read and digested, our approach cultivates an experience that is moment-focused: It is meant to enhance your impression of the feature work in all of the ineffable ways—the tickle in the brain, the flutter in the heart.

We have done our best to stir the waters and bring to the surface lesser-known works of authors—forgoing William Butler Yeats's (1839-1922) "The Second Coming" and instead publishing his essays "The Body of the Father Christian Rosencrux" and "William Blake and the Imagination", or bringing back to the forefront women writers like Aphra Behn (1640-1689) who have not been given their due in the syllabi of classical curricula. We at Lazuli want to separate from the echo chamber of works that are in ubiquitous circulation and assumed to define what counts as "good literature".

In reflection of the dramatic stage format of *Intimate Things*, we have chosen excerpts from Wallace Stevens's little-known early play *Carlos Among the Candles* (1917) that uses the medium of the stage to offer poetry in patches, and from Oscar Wilde's *Salomé* (1893), with the princess's repetitive, chilling decree to "give me the head of Jokanaan", providing an interesting character study in relationship to Courie's rendition of Heloise. Other selections here include poetry that reflects desperation, forbidden affections, the intertwining of death and love in the human heart. These works play with how romantic roles slide into one another, how gender is conceived in relationships over changing eras, and how one makes sense of all the angles of *Intimate Things* that are but limned outlines of emotions unbounded. The pairings are meant to illuminate your reading in some way—be it via a similar or contrasting structure, a tonal quality, a thematic connection, or a character double or foil—and, with thanks to the author, Laylage Courie, for her additional recommendations, we have collected this visceral experience in a volume to be shared.

Intimate Things is a work that asks one to suspend a desire for stark outlines and rather to live freely in the landscape of imagination. The selected literary pairings will open and make the mind comfortable in this sensibility. We humbly present to you this curated reading experience.

—Sakina B. Fakhri

Intimate Things

by
Laylage Courie

Intimate Things

In memory of Sabina Maya Angel.
— L. Courie

Characters

Heloise
Abelard
Swell Henry (a man played by a woman)

Place

ACT I: The Dialogues of Heloise & Abelard
at the Paraclete
An imaginary lecture/demonstration.

ACT II: Sic et Non
A lecture with interruptions.

ACT III: Indeed words were few
A lonely man at a bar.

Time

The suspended present

Act I
The Dialogues of Heloise & Abelard at the Paraclete

(SWELL HENRY appears to be the Director, who for budgetary reasons is also the stagehand, of this play.)

(The stage makes some small pretense of being an austere rhetorical school/convent in 12th century France. It is possibly set only with chairs and microphones, in the form of a panel discussion, along with, as example, a garland of fake roses, a small gothic arch resting on a table-top, a color print-out of a religious stained glass window on a folding easel or... etc. ABELARD might enter, ask SWELL HENRY for water. SWELL HENRY might bring two plastic cups on a lunch tray along with a cheap wine bottle wrapped like a basket. He imagines the bottle is a rustic earthenware jug. It is the best he can do.)

(Etcetera.)

Scene One
He plays the lion in his house[1]

(ABELARD is alone. HELOISE enters.)

ABELARD

Let us sit facing the sun. I like the sun in my eyes. With the sun in my eyes, the present, now, becomes golden. Like a memory. The sun will not always fall so fully on our faces: forehead, cheeks, collar bones, or, permit me to observe, décolletage. What fine wrists. I like. The way the sun suggests. I sprawl. With indifferent languor. Like a beast.

(HELOISE sits.)

(End of Scene.)

Scene Two
SHE CANNOT BE EQUALLY WITH MEN AND GOD[2]

(HELOISE speaks to ABELARD without looking at him.)

HELOISE

He says: "A part of you is always alone." Isolated, immune, removed, distant, alienated, separate, detached. Faraway. Solitary. Cut-off. Deserted, desolate, remote, estranged, at-odds, divided. Uninvolved. Indifferent. Impassive. Shut-down...

ABELARD

Maybe...

(HELOISE looks at ABELARD.)

HELOISE

I'm not alone.
I'm just not with him.
I'm with someone else.
Inside.

(ABELARD nods.)

(End of Scene.)

Scene Three
SHE HAS SLIPPED OFF HER DRESS[3]

(HELOISE speaks to herself. ABELARD is not listening.)

HELOISE

This is where the story begins. Here. In this room. Finding the dust and lost change beneath the mattress, behind the bed. I won't toss what I find. I will spit on it, murmur a few magic words, and shape it into a beast. A beast with the power of a lion and the grace. Of a winged horse. I will tend her. Lovingly.

(End of Scene.)

Scene Four
NIGHT AFTER NIGHT ON HER NARROW BED SHE SEEKS TRUE LOVE[4]

(HELOISE and ABELARD speak to each other.)

HELOISE
I feel like a girl who has come to tell her father some thing. The thing is precious to her but as she begins to speak it, she feels ashamed.

ABELARD
Because it is wrong?

HELOISE
Too precious to speak?

(Pause.)

ABELARD
May I ask if you experience problems of a sexual nature?

HELOISE
Yes. Oh yes. But. Not really.

(Pause.)

ABELARD
Would you say you feel incomplete or unfulfilled? Needy or insistent? Empty? Or unsatisfied?

Heloise

I would say I feel hungry. With a hunger no man has the imagination to fill.

(End of Scene.)

Scene Five
THE HEAVENLY BRIDEGROOM TORMENTS HER WITH TRIBULATIONS[5]

(HELOISE speaks to SWELL HENRY.)

HELOISE
We don't discuss it. No. It is simply chained to our legs like a feral dog.

(End of Scene.)

Scene Six
The Importance of the problem is matched by the subtlety of his solution[6]

(ABELARD speaks to the audience. HELOISE listens.)

ABELARD

I want to talk about "imagination." I want to talk about what I imagine at night. I imagine trees. Very old trees. Common trees. Oak trees, poplar trees, sycamore. I imagine a tree's life in reverse. I imagine: twigs shriveling into branches into trunk. Filament roots sucked back into the tap. Solar flares, dirt, rain hurl as a century-old tree is compressed into a sapling, a sapling standing like an adolescent, arms lifted towards heaven at the still hole in the center of a hurricane before it is sucked back into the earth.

The winds settles around upheaved ground. Where a seed nestles. A seed nestles in the earth.

Explosive.

(End of Scene.)

Scene Seven
FROM THE ENDS OF THE EARTH HE CALLS WHEN HIS HEART IS IN ANGUISH[7]

(HELOISE speaks to ABELARD.)

HELOISE

Do you dream about the wind? Do you dream that the wind tears through your hair? Lifts your arms and parts your legs? The wind smears your face against your skull. You look like a satyr with your face smeared against your skull. You are lifted. On your back. The stars whirl nearer, nearer and you laugh. You double over, laughing. Doubled-over, you are too heavy and you fall. You smash against the ground. Then something else. I can't remember. A departure. A going forth into darkness. Along a path so smooth I think it must be paved with water.

(End of Scene.)

Scene Eight
THE MORE HE POSSESSES THAT WHICH CAN BE LOST
THE GREATER THE FEAR WHICH TORMENTS HIM[8]

(ABELARD speaks to the audience. HELOISE listens.)

ABELARD

I used to dream of water. Flood. The walls of the oratory rising like cliffs around a lake where the pews are drowned. Fish leaped before the altar of the fisher of men. Drowned birds dredge the alcoves, butting against mold-blackened saints. Boatmen engage in for-profit ferrying up and down the aisles. Rats scramble, snouts poked above the flood. Paddling rats. You don't think that's funny? Rats scurrying in water against a torrential flood? The faithful clambering up the bas-relief? Dangling from arches like clusters of grapes? Garlanding the pointed windows like a profane host? I'll admit I hesitated to love anyone. Whenever love rose in my body, yes, like a flood, I remembered that everyone—especially the everyone that I loved—would die. Love. How do people bear it? Forget "betrayal." Forget "separation." Even "The Best Scenario"—a long and happy life—ends tragically.

It was hard, knowing that, to embrace rapture with all-welcoming arms.

(End of Scene.)

Scene Nine
THE TONGUE IS A SMALL MEMBER OF THE BODY BUT HOW VAST A FOREST IT CAN SET ALIGHT[9]

ABELARD
Tell me about him.

HELOISE
About sleeping with him? I liked it.

ABELARD
Trying to sleep with him?

HELOISE
Yes. I'd like that, too. Yes.

ABELARD
Because it would take a long time.

HELOISE
I'd like his hands on me. Their furiousness. Their increasing furiousness. Their desperation.

ABELARD
What does it feel like.

HELOISE
Stillness in the center of a hurricane.

ABELARD
No it doesn't.

HELOISE

Yes it does.

ABELARD

A dry wind through blanched grasses.

HELOISE

(Pause.) The rustling wind across open fields.

ABELARD

Like that. Exactly.

(End of Scene.)

Scene Ten

HE LOOKS ON WINE WHEN IT GLOWS AND SPARKLES IN THE CUP[10]

(HELOISE speaks to the audience while ABELARD listens.)
(HELOISE smokes.)

HELOISE
Would you like one?

ABELARD
I like that your lips don't leave stains on the cigarette tip.

HELOISE
I don't rouge my lips.

ABELARD
Yes. That's why there are no stains.

HELOISE
Why don't you just say "I like that you don't rouge your lips"?

ABELARD
Because I wouldn't mind if you did rouge them. I like that when the cigarette comes out of your mouth, it is unsoiled. Moistened. But white.

(End of Scene.)

Scene Eleven
SHE DISDAINS TO RISE FROM THE BED OF HER CONTEMPLATION[11]

(HELOISE speaks to the audience while ABELARD listens.)

HELOISE

Shall I tell you of my only love? Who interrupts my dreams? He interrupts he is gold and husked. I peel the husk. He feels good in my hands. Sun-warmed. Thick. Silked and sticky. Kernels pop between my teeth before he plow tills the field, its ridge in the furrow grind of some god beneath the belly, from the slashed stalk splitting its sheathe. I am unsheathed for dawn scattering its kernels of gold from the sky into the bed into the womb.

ABELARD

That bloody animal.

HELOISE

Yes.

(End of Scene.)

Scene Twelve
He gathers each blossom as it comes to mind and creates a single bunch[12]

(Abelard speaks to the audience. Heloise is not listening.)

Abelard

This is where the story begins. Scraping fluff and coinage from my pockets, shaping them with spit and a few magic words into an animal. A magical beast. "This is my life," I say. The virility of a satyr. The fierceness of a bull. The wise inconstancy of a centaur. Ah Bacchanal! This is the story I tell. This is the myth I make.

(End of Scene.)

Scene Thirteen
Whoever sits in solitude shall have only the Heart to fight against[13]

(HELOISE and ABELARD face the audience)

HELOISE

Are you unsatisfied? Discontent? Saddened? Lost on the tumultuous winds? Are you equipped for the journey? Are you without compass? Have you lost your sense of direction? Sex? Life?

ABELARD

At night. Before the sun is set. Twilight.

HELOISE

As the sun is setting.

ABELARD

I wander. Windows illuminated before curtains are drawn. I see the colors of walls. The decoration of rooms. I've never once seen two people kissing. Twilight, as the sun sets, don't you want to sit close with someone dear in your arms? As the day, the whole day, departs? And kiss them? Kiss them as the last glances of light are thrown off interior mirrors like the reflection of passing birds?

HELOISE

You walk the streets.

ABELARD

At night. Curtains drawn. On the streets. I look at the trees. Two hundred years old. Lining the streets. Their girth. The wondrous complexity of their branching. I run my hands along their trunks.

HELOISE
I saw two people kissing. They looked at each other with heavy eyes. His hand was inside her blouse. I could see the cotton crease and stretch and rise. Her legs parted as if she had forgotten them. Her eyes were as heavy as water. I saw a girl once. She stood before her uncle. She looked at him, then at her knees. He sat at his desk with his back to her.

ABELARD
Did she want to tell him something?

HELOISE
Was that the day she found blood on her thighs? There are several reasons for that, aren't there? Some of them a girl wouldn't tell her father about, would she? What would he think of her?

ABELARD
He would feel sad for her. He would feel sad because he would feel the pain of the whole world rushing towards her like thousands of sharp knives.

(End of Scene.)

Scene Fourteen
Although her body is cloistered her mind still loves things outside and pursues them[14]

(Heloise speaks to the audience. Abelard is not listening.)

Heloise

What do I like?

A resonant voice. Sounding like the drum of hands on hollowed wood.

Strong hands. The hands that could hollow a boat or a drum out of wood. Hands that can do delicate work with simple tools.

The look on a man's face when he's doing delicate work. When he's concentrating.

I like a man who is sure in the water. I like to see arms, chest, breaking the surface of the water. The line of the water at his hip, at his thighs. His body, surfacing. The light breaks off his body. He shakes his head. Glass is thrown. I weep. Oh penetrating beauty. How can I ever hold you? I will never hold you. I weep for such temporaries. Glass in my skin. In my eyes.

What do I like?

HELOISE (CONT'D)
A man who can stand at a threshold. Step over that threshold without hesitation. As necessary. As it became inevitable. Not without sorrow. With dignity. I like the man who, when he hovers at a threshold, looks back, for only the fraction needed to sign, beyond all words: Good bye. Fare well.

My only love.

(HELOISE looks at ABELARD.)

(End of Scene.)

Scene Fifteen
Always they seek the forbidden and desire what is denied[15]

ABELARD

Tell me about your friend.

HELOISE

The nun and the philosopher obscure themselves in robes of night.

ABELARD

(Furious.) This is where the story begins. Where we take the fluff, lint, coinage of our days and make of them some kind of myth.

(End of Scene.)

Scene Sixteen

She would rather be experienced in bed than seen at a table[16]

(Heloise and Abelard face off.)

Abelard

Ravish me.

Heloise

A fantasy.

Abelard

If you will.

Heloise

A man in a garden. I can tell a lot about a man from his manner in a garden. Does he stroll purposefully, or meander? When a flower is fragrant, in what way do his hands lift a bud to his mouth? The way he asks if I'd like to sit. Does he lead me, or merely offer? Is he assured? Does he try to please? His command of the situation.

Abelard

Shall I tell you what I am like?

Heloise

What you yourself are like?

Abelard

Of course. The woman with me. This makes a difference. Imagine, for instance, it is you. It is late afternoon. Autumn.

The light is gold at the edges of your hair. It is warm and you wear clothes like that. That fall open. I am aware of the bare skin beneath your throat. Perhaps I do not notice the roses. Their fragrance. I am a man of intention. I watch you. You cross your arms. You smile, generously. Such a generous smile. I say "Will you sit on this bench for a moment, where the last light falls?" You answer... what do you answer?

HELOISE

Yes.

ABELARD

And you sit, right in the middle of the bench, and I do not know where I should sit. So I sit in front of you, positioned to look out, into the cool, gold light, and also at you, surreptitiously. I speak concisely but my attention, really, remains on you. The distance between us. It is not so large because I am tall when I sit. If you will but stay, leaned forward, with your elbows on your knees, I think I would like to touch two fingers to your chin, lean in, and kiss you. I intend it gently but, alas, I kiss you and. My body. Suspends. It is as if a stone hits the pool of my body, here, at my solar plexus and from that "here" I ripple out. Suspense. Suspend. Exquisitely. I kiss you. Your ankles uncross and my knee slips between yours. Such languor in your body. Your body falling open. Softening. The languor of breezes in meadows. A woman being kissed. You. Kissed.

HELOISE
Your eyes. Gold-edged in the light.

ABELARD
Your skin, beneath the lines of your clothes, cream.

HELOISE
Stay with me. Stay.

(End of Scene.)

Scene Seventeen
ALL MIRACLES ARE PERFORMED EITHER IN LONELY OR IN HIDDEN PLACES[17]

HELOISE
If only.
Your mouth...

ABELARD
Shhhh.

HELOISE
... here.

ABELARD
It is time to go.

(End of Scene.)

Scene Eighteen

AN EMBRACE IN THE ARMS OF FAITH FOR HE WHO ACTS DIVINELY IN THE GLORIOUS FLESH OF A VIRGIN WHICH HE ASSUMED FROM THE PARACLETE[18]

(Silence.)

(The distance between HELOISE and ABELARD and.)

(The space between their bodies.)

(The shape of the space between their bodies.)

(More present than they are.)

(HELOISE exits.)

(End of Scene.)

Scene Nineteen
DO YOU NOT KNOW THAT YOUR BODY IS A SHRINE OF THE IN-DWELLING HOLY SPIRIT?[19]

(ABELARD, in HELOISE's absence, speaks to the audience.)

ABELARD

Love without language. I will tell you about her body. I will tell you about her body as I lay her on the bed. Softly. As if she were a girl. I lowered her to the bed. The sheets were gold. Her body was white. The color of milk. Her hair. All over her body. Dark. The white rocks of the river dark with algae. No. Love without language. The long shapes of her legs. As they opened. Opening. Parting. I parted them. My hands gentle at her knees, along the inside of her thighs. Yes. Love without language. I will tell you about her body. I will tell you how her hips lifted, her back arched. I will tell you about her breasts pushing upwards as her head fell back. I will tell you about her hair between my fingers on my tongue in my mouth. I will tell you about her eyes when she was lost. How deep. The depth of her eyes as her mind died and she was only aware of her body. The depth of her eyes, dark, bottomless, instinctual. Let no man go there. Let no man. But we plunge in. We cannot help ourselves. We plunge inside. And I held her to me. I pulled her close into my chest. These are the mysteries. These are the mysteries. Love without language. I will tell you. I will tell you about the dark places. The dark places when the soul inhabits the body. The deep places, then, in our eyes. When her eyes close, she sleeps. What is it dies? Endlessly? Endless? What is it? Inside?

(End of Scene.)

Scene Twenty
THIS IS NOT OFFERING A KISS BUT PROFERRING A CUP[20]

(ABELARD re-lights HELOISE's cigarette from before.)

(Smokes.)

(Stubs out.)

(Exits.)

(Ash in a dish on an empty stage.)

(From which smoke rises.)

(For a long time.)

(End of Scene.)

END OF ACT I

Laylage Courie

Act II
Sic Et Non

(SWELL HENRY lectures. ABELARD listens. HELOISE is not present.)

(SWELL HENRY displays supporting exhibits on a screen. The exhibits will become less and less relevant. The Empire State Building should eventually appear. See Act III.)

SWELL HENRY

Abelard and Heloise lived in Medieval France. He was the greatest logician/philosopher of the 12th century. She was renowned in her own time for her knowledge and understanding of classical literature. Abelard seduced Heloise when hired by her Uncle as her tutor. When she became pregnant, he secretly married her and stashed her in a convent, where they continued to have passionate rendez-vous. When Heloise's Uncle discovered he had been deceived by the formerly celibate scholar in his own house, he hired henchmen to castrate Abelard in his sleep. There ended Eros between Heloise & Abelard. He became a monk, she, a nun. Their letters begin some ten years later, after Abelard spent a brief time serving as the Father Confessor to Heloise and her nuns at the Paraclete—the school he founded and later gave to Heloise for her convent. The letters begin with a letter from Heloise to Abelard full of longing, anger, and betrayal. She claims Abelard had not spoken personally to her the entire time they co-habited at the Paraclete.

ABELARD

In love you will float. In a small boat. Over unfathomable

depths. A lake silver brimmed to the horizon. But allow. Allow yourself to rise. From the lake's surface. Its shore will become apparent. Its silvery surface will grow smaller and smaller, until it is resolved into a coin. Engraved with a boat. In which two people are vaguely supposed. To sit.

Swell Henry

In love you will float. In a small boat. Over unfathomable depths. A lake silver brimmed to the horizon. But allow. Allow yourself to rise. From the lake's surface. Its shore will become apparent. Its silvery surface will grow smaller and smaller, until it is resolved into a coin. Engraved with a boat. In which two people are vaguely supposed. To sit.

Abelard

I would write more things to you but a few words instruct a wise man. Intention is all and intention is lacking. Indifferenter (indifferently) scibilitas (knowability). Sic et non. What more?[21]

Logic has made me hated by the world.[22] The storm may rage but I am unshaken though the winds may blow they leave me unmoved; for the rock of my foundation stands firm.[23]

Swell Henry

The coin can be treasured, pocketed, stolen, lost, or spent. It is evident that love must be drowned in or resolved with this perspective. It is impossible to float tranquilly upon it for long.

Afterwards, what? Dive back into the deception with someone new? What "real thing" remains once passion has died, the lake is demoted to coin? In his letters to Heloise, Abelard says "God". I can't blame Heloise for her frustration with him. It is possible she had seen Abelard only once after her Uncle's henchmen castrated him in his sleep. When he signed her into a convent. Imagine that: Heloise, the abbess and a sister or two, meet Abelard in a small receiving chamber. Abelard is in a state of shock. Heloise represents his humiliation and shame. She is "she-who-I-can-no-longer-fuck." He thinks, at this time, that a eunuch befouls the eyes of God. His humiliation and self-disgust must be extreme. Any glance between Heloise & Abelard is as intense and as forsaken as the glance between Orpheus and Eurydice. As I imagine it, Heloise is both Orpheus & Eurydice, Abelard the mirror in which she glances at herself. The act of being seen by her beloved as no-longer-beloved is violent for her. It is the moment that her life is severed, her passion dismembered. Abelard's dismemberment preexists his meeting Heloise. The loss of Heloise is merely a symptom of the violence. His inner turmoil obliterates any other emotion. He is not really in the moment, the last moment, with her. He cannot be. He is in shock. She sees, through him, herself drawn into the underworld. Heloise, looking back at her beloved who no longer sees her as beloved, sees herself, sinking from the earth through soil into the land of shades. She takes her vows. Before him, because he did not trust her to go through with it.

The knife's cut, for Heloise, is not clean. Passion was full in her mouth. The knife pried her jaw open and snatched it away. Unlike Abelard, she is hungry.

When Abelard replies to Heloise's first letter to address her "old perpetual complaint against God concerning the manner of our entry into religious life" he uses erotic metaphors to describe the nobility of her cloistered life. Heloise's lover is no longer Abelard, it is the Lord. How blessed is she! A chunk of Letter 5 analyzes a Canticle about a European King's Ethiopian wife. Her black skin looks less lovely, but is soft, subtle, and loveliest to experience in bed. The Ethiopian bride—Heloise's soul cloaked in the outwardly unattractive life of a nun—is the superior consort, most pleasing in the bed of the Lord. Heloise has entered a sacred chamber where she is sublimely embraced by the Lord. Abelard humbly addresses his Lord's bride. The eunuch serves his master's queen.

I laugh when I read Heloise's response. She nobly agrees to restrain herself from continuing complaint. She instead humbly petitions Abelard for advice on convent "Rules": what clothing and underwear should sisters wear suitable to their fragile bodies and menstrual cycle? Should sisters offer Christian hospitality to men and eat at table with them or is that inviting temptation? She asks, too, if sisters should drink wine given it "encourages sensuality". Yes, I project my preferred subtext: I don't want Heloise & Abelard to slip too easily into cloister banter. He responds to her plea for personal discourse with lofty sexual metaphors about "knowing" God? She asks him to consider what she wears under her habit, her volatile libido. Knowing, as we do from his letter, what his "uncontrollable desire did" with her in the "corner of the refectory" dedicated to the "the most holy virgin" while Heloise was disguised as a nun, ("I, repeat, you know how shamelessly we behaved on that occasion in so hallowed a place," writes Abelard), her questions are sharp.

Nevertheless, it isn't titillation I look for in the *Letters of Abelard & Heloise*. I read to know what they meant each to the other when passion was lost to them. Abelard addresses Heloise as his "beloved", "once dearest to me in the world, now dearest to me in Christ." Is this deep-seated feeling or proper style? Letters of the period (according to the introduction) were always written in a grandiose, literary style. What do his addresses signify? I am alarmed by what reads as estrangement. What comfort does Abelard draw knowing Heloise prays for him as he endures heresy charges, book-burnings, and assassination attempts? "I can find nowhere to rest or even to live; a fugitive and wanderer I carry everywhere the curse of Cain, forever tormented..." he writes. When accusations against him peak, when "logic" makes him "hated by the world," he writes a confession of faith to her. It feels urgent, almost personal. Abelard trades erotic Heloise for Heloise-the-sacred-bride. He expects her to intercede on his behalf on judgment day. "A man's wrongdoing will be wiped out by the entreaties of his wife."

Heloise? Did Abelard's presence always dwell quietly beneath or above or within her practical and scholarly work? Did her love diminish in intensity? I imagine that it did, that time brought perspective. The lake, if not a coin, became a pond that her life flowed into, then out of, on its way to the sea. Perhaps she found quietude after his death, when news of him, words from him, or even his arrival were no longer possible. Her heart, full of longing towards nothing of this earth, slowly emptied itself of worldly passion.

It is desirable to imagine that for both Heloise and Abelard, a meta-reality co-existed with the trials and details of their daily lives, and that each could retreat to it. This meta-reality undoubtedly contained a presence they called God, but it also contained an image of the other as soul's mate traveling parallel towards a single vanishing point, a familiar to be finally met in the here-beyond. It is tempting, necessary, to imagine this.

I read Heloise and Abelard to learn how the soul loves beyond Eros. My edition notes that both were familiar with Cicero's De Amicitia, a treatise which founded an ideal relationship of "disinterested love". Both Heloise & Abelard believed in an ideal love of devotion, "disinterestedness" that transcended marriage and eroticism. Reading that, I am irritated. When the erotic element is lost, their relationship drastically changes! I want these great lovers to instruct, not on how the ideal is lived abstractly across time and space sublimated in the fantastical bliss of eternal union, but humanly, viscerally, embedded in the everyday real. I wish Heloise & Abelard had lived more intimately or written more often. I am disappointed that they do not teach me how the soul's love, after passion, dwells humbly, deeply, and contentedly, in our common world.

They do not tell me that love of the soul dwells humbly, contentedly, in our world.

ABELARD[24]
I will open my mouth in parables.

> It is a noteworthy quality to love the truth in the words, not the words themselves. For what use is a golden key if it cannot unlock what we desire? And what is wrong with a wooden key, if it can unlock what we desire, when we wish nothing but to open what is closed?
>
> ---
>
> Although there is no place in the entire universe that is entirely empty and not filled either with air or some other body, still we say that a box in which we perceive nothing by sight is empty.
>
> ---
>
> If there be anything left, you shall burn it with fire.
>
> ---
>
> A sentence is true if things stand in the way it says, and things make sentences true or false in virtue of the way they are, and nothing further is required.

(SWELL HENRY turns off his projector. While he puts on his coat, these words appear on the exhibit screen. They are cast by

a projector held by HELOISE, standing in the audience. SWELL HENRY does not see HELOISE or the words.)

(Projected words, one line at a time:)

A TRICKLING FONT.

BASIN SMOOTH AND UNADORNED.

HELOISE (GARDEN) SPLASHED UPON.

WHOLE, GLISTENING, SPLASHED UPON.

HER CALF, CROOKED OVER RIM, SWINGS.

LIKE A CENSER.

ATTAR OF ROSE. WORMWOOD.

LISTEN AGAIN PLEASE: THE TRICKLING FONT.

STUTTERING SPILLAGE AS

SHE EMERGES.

HELOISE.

HEAD BOWED.

SHE EMERGES (BASIN)

HANDS CLUTCH RIM

BACK ARCH REVEALS

WINGS

(HERS)

FEATHERED WITH STONES.

TREMORING.

MONSTROUS AND IDLE.

Abelard

(Calm.)
Hand towards hat plumed with swords. Draw. Advancing.

Heloise's song

(Singing:)
Nominatissima,
choose shoes soled thin as eyelids
I implore you to the chapel at dawn.
There will bed reveal what my heart now hides.
Let the sweet fountain of yourself bubble over
Who can deny you are buried in me?

(SWELL HENRY exits in his coat.)

(ABELARD, on stage, looks out at HELOISE, in the audience, holding a projector of light.)

Abelard

Lo I escaped far away and found a refuge in the wilderness. I took myself off to a lonely spot I had known before.[25] A tree pierced the sky like a ragged thorn. Memory is the most treacherous tempter, reverie mangling austere practice. Purity is allotted only to our bones.

ABELARD	HELOISE
(Calm:) My love, which brought us both to sin, should be called lust, not love. I took my fill of my wretched pleasures in you, and this was the sum total of my love. Mourn for your savior and redeemer, not for your corrupter and fornicator. It was he who truly loved you, not I. Farewell in Christ in Christ fare well and live in Christ. [26]	*(Blank shouting:)* My love, which brought us both to sin, should be called lust, not love? I took my fill of my wretched pleasures in you, and this was the sum total of my love? Mourn for your savior and redeemer, not for your corrupter and fornicator? It was he who truly loved you, not I? Farewell in Christ in Christ fare well and live in Christ?

HELOISE

Love is a black river that runs towards death. The waters are cold and dark. Only a beast could cross such a river. We are not delicate, strong enough. The water is too cold. Too swift.

END OF ACT II

Laylage Courie

Act III
Indeed Words Were Few

(Swell Henry enters a bar near the Empire State Building.)

(Swell Henry removes his coat.)

(He selects a bottle and a glass from the bar, then sits.)

Swell Henry

(A toast:)
Oh my radiant sunrise oh my radiant sun. She has four thorns. Four thorns radial from the wheel of her mind. They crown her like rays emanating from a Madonna. She is not a Madonna. The thorns are her own. Her hair as red as blood. From the four thorns? No. She has placed the thorns carefully. She does not bleed. Her smile is sad but her eyes are as calm as oceans.

(A toast:)
Oceans.

(Soliloquy:)
I hear the wind. Not swiftly. Not in gusts. Continuously. It does not let up. The wind tosses tin airplanes and boats. It tosses bits of paper and sea froth. It crosses vast distances. I hear it because I am born-in-air. I am born-in-air and I hear the wind blowing, not just around this building, through these streets, but high in the stratosphere. Because I am born-in-air, my heart is an aircraft with a small, straight beacon light, navigating up there. In the winds. I am that insignificant. That insignificant and that free. Tied to nothing. Tossed

in turbulence. Blown through sky. What a joyous thing is man! Buckled in his little tin can, tossed in the unnavigable, indifferent wind. On his way. Somewhere.

Of course the tin can has wings. That's why one can laugh, one can go-with-the-flow, so to speak, having wings.

Tonight I'm a real cloud stopper. Did I say that? Did I say cloud? Crowd? Crowd pleaser. I'm a real pleaser of crowds. Here's the bottle. And the glass. And the bar.
Have you noticed that no one's tending the bar?

(Calling out:)
There is no one tending the bar!

(To Audience:)
If you come up here I am not going to make your drink.

No. I do not golish plasses or drix minks.

(To self:)
Did I say that?

(To Audience:)
I do not do those things, I'm saying. I sit here. At the bar. With a whole bottle to myself. So I don't really need a bartender. I'm a pleaser of clouds. A real cloud pleaser. Clouds cross vast distances, oceans, on the great winds, to hover over me. The winds. Hear them?

(Pause to listen.)

They are very high. You can hear them particularly at the top of a tall building. The Empire State Building, for example, which, I believe, is still standing. Right over there. Is it still standing? Yes. I believe it is. It is standing. And—as I was saying—if YOU stand at the top of it and if it is not too crowded and if you aren't too tired or. If you are. Very, very tired. You can stand very still on the top of it and feel it moving, every so slightly. Swaying like a woman imagining a dance from a long, long time ago.

No. That's not how it sways. It is not introverted, it does not sway inside itself. It sways against an outside force. Yes. The Empire State Building sways—as I was saying—against the wind. You can hear the wind there, if you are still and tired or not very tired and there are no clouds. I mean crowds. You can feel the subterranean hydraulic shifts balancing one thousand four hundred and fifty-four feet of steel, glass, duct work, office furniture, plumbing and wire, against the force of air. You can feel the shifting under your feet. You can see the view—the pan-o-rama, so to speak, move. An engineering feat. Vertiginous. And—as I was saying—you can hear the force it adjusts to. You can hear the wind. Constant. A wordless breath. Not menacing. Just indifferent. Just terribly terribly forceful and indifferent. You hear it and you are apt to feel, surely, that you have miss-stepped. That you have tread on inhuman, therefore sacred, ground. You were not meant to stand here. To be this high. You are a mere man, meant to stand, awestruck, beneath the altar of the cathedral, looking up in wonder at its nether reaches. Only great men—Master Builders, Michelangelo—are meant to stand at the tops of cathedrals. Because God—or whatever—is supposed to dwell Up There. But here you are, higher than any cathedral, with a touch of vertigo, watching.

The clouds swiftly pass.

The sun, that ancient clock, arc.
The city sprawl over three states.

The Atlantic crash over the horizon.

And you don't hear God. No. You hear the wind. Do you hear it?

(Pause for listening.)

You know what's worst? No one's painted the ceiling for you. When you stand at the top of the Empire State Building and look up, the beauty of the archangels does not take your breath away. No. Your breath is punched out of your gut. If you fall to your knees it is out of sheer dizziness, not awe. Survival instinct yanks your gaze out of the wild blue yonder before you are lost. Forever.

Did I say that? I can't believe I said that. It is a phrase, a phrase out of Gone with the Wind. Or something. It is a ridiculous, melodramatic phrase. Can you be lost, forever? Wouldn't you eventually stumble upon some place you'd been before? Or your soul. Your spirit. Can it be lost forever? No. I do not think so. If it lasts forever. If that, then it will find its home there. It will find its home somewhere in forever. Or it will be where it is and not want to be anywhere else and so it won't be lost anymore because it won't want to go anywhere. Or.

(SWELL HENRY looks up, falters, and falls to his knees.)

Ver-ti-gi-nous.

(He clambers back up.)

And now, ladies and gentleman, a real cloud stopper: The Staircase Genius. Who has a pair of dice. He is flanked to left and right by winged, radiant Madonnas offering safety nets like chalices to the sky. Beneath him there is ocean, and above him, the sun circles and falls, agelessly. Above him, high, high above him, the sound of the wind.

The sound of the wind not speaking, not calling to him.

No. The wind:

> born out of pressure and solar flares
> pulled pole to pole, magnetic north to south
> cooled over fissured ice fields
> run rampant over the unhindered plains
> pushing eastward across great lakes, mountain ranges
> to the eastern seaboard
> the wind, I say, whipping towards the Atlantic

snags its hem on the nails of New York where loose threads of it gust through the street corridors. This is where the Staircase Genius begins his climb. The Staircase Genius staggers back. But he is not discouraged. Yes.

No. The silliness. Wind. Cloth. Let the wind be as it is. Irreducible. Unrestricted by metaphor, cathedrals, skyscrapers. Hear it.

(Pause for listening. SWELL HENRY regroups.)

The Staircase Genius hears the wind. Bracing himself, he casts

two dice on the stair. The number: three. He leaps three sheets to the Three steps into the wind. He picks up the dice. He casts them. His life is a baffling dream.
The stairs go up up up insurmountably. The sky is radiant and then it is dark, in quick succession. Sometimes he is blinded, and sometimes, in darkness, he is blind.

The genius of the Staircase Genius is that he does not despair, he does not fret, as he climbs this kind of stair. The Staircase Genius looks up up up straight into the sky and when he does so he does not fall to his knees and he does not suffer from vertigo. He sees the sun, crossing. He notes its position. His eyes blink with the modesty of straightforward calculation. He looks at the stair immediately before him and casts his dice. With the efficacy of an engineer. He leaps forward.

(Fierce, to self:)
But I, I am born-in-air. I cast my dice against the wind and leap after them. Perhaps I will fall to the ocean. Perhaps, I will ascend, toes pointed like a saint's, face radiant like an idiot's, into the yild blue wonder.

Did I say that?

(Cold resolve:)
Then what will now happen is: the liquid I have drunk from this glass will, as I tilt my head back to drink... flow, in slow motion, from my mouth back into the glass. When I lower the glass to the table (as if lifting it in reverse) I will already be holding the bottle directly over the glass. The liquid will waft, like a genii, up from the glass into the bottle. When I set the bottle down, it will be full. A miracle. The evening will go backwards. Oh my radiant sunrise oh my radiant sun she has

four thorns four thorns radial from the wheel of her mind...
and so forth, in reverse. Everything. Backwards. Backwards.
Until...
Until?

Were I saint this bottle will be full. Were I idiot it will full, though you might only see the fool, dribbling spit down his chin. But in truth? Though born-in-air, if I leap after the dice, the wind will blot me against the sun like an apparition for an instant only. Then, I will fall, a clot of earth, out of the sky. The bottle will be empty.

(Toasts:)
She has four thorns four thorns radial from the wheel of her mind. They crown her like rays emanating from a Madonna. She is not a Madonna. The thorns are her own. Her hair as red as blood. She has placed the thorns carefully. She does not bleed. She does not bleed. Her smile is sad but her eyes are as calm as oceans.

(A toast:)
Whatever a lover gives to a lover, what more?[27]

(A toast:)
Indeed, words were few.

(To self:)
But I made them many by re-reading them.[28]

> *(He is going to toast again, but the bottle is empty.)*
> *(He considers the bottle.)*

(He tries it... going backwards: he lifts the empty glass to his

*mouth. He lowers the glass to the table, lifting the bottle back
over it—the gesture of drinking/pouring in absolute reverse.
When the bottle is again poised over the glass he stares intently
at the space between them with excruciating hopefulness: for a
moment he believes liquid will rise back into the bottle.)*

*(Speaking the following is arduous at first, but builds in speed
and eloquence, making some kind of sense:)*

Swell Henry

By many them made I but few were words indeed.
More what lover a to gives lover a whatever.
Oceans as calm as are eyes her but sad is smile her bleed not
does she bleed not does she.
Carefully.
Thorns the placed has she blood as red as hair
her own her are thorns the Madonna a not is she
Madonna a from emanating rays like her crown
Mind her
Wheel radial thorns four thorns four has she
sun radiant my
oh rise sun radiant my
oh

(Stillness.)

SWELL HENRY (CONT'D)
Love is a black river that runs towards death, that black tree charring the sky as if lightning slashed out of the earth. Purity is allotted only to our bones.

END

LITERARY
PAIRINGS

'No worst, there is none. Pitched past pitch of grief.'
(1878)

By Gerard Manley Hopkins

No worst, there is none. Pitched past pitch of grief,
More pangs will, schooled at forepangs, wilder wring.
Comforter, where, where is your comforting?
Mary, mother of us, where is your relief?
My cries heave, herds-long; huddle in a main, a chief
Woe, wórld-sorrow; on an áge-old anvil wince and sing —
Then lull, then leave off. Fury had shrieked 'No lingering! Let me be fell: force I must be brief.'

  O the mind, mind has mountains; cliffs of fall
Frightful, sheer, no-man-fathomed. Hold them cheap
May who ne'er hung there. Nor does long our small
Durance deal with that steep or deep. Here! creep,
Wretch, under a comfort serves in a whirlwind: all
Life death does end and each day dies with sleep.

Sonnet 12: When I do count the clock that tells the time
(1609)

By William Shakespeare

When I do count the clock that tells the time,
And see the brave day sunk in hideous night;
When I behold the violet past prime,
And sable curls all silver'd o'er with white;
When lofty trees I see barren of leaves
Which erst from heat did canopy the herd,
And summer's green all girded up in sheaves
Borne on the bier with white and bristly beard,
Then of thy beauty do I question make,
That thou among the wastes of time must go,
Since sweets and beauties do themselves forsake
And die as fast as they see others grow;
   And nothing 'gainst Time's scythe can make defence
   Save breed, to brave him when he takes thee hence.

ELEGY
(1586)

By Chidiock Tichborne

My prime of youth is but a frost of cares;
My feast of joy is but a dish of pain,
My crop of corn is but a field of tares,
And all my good is but vain hope of gain:
The day is past, and yet I saw no sun,
And now I live, and now my life is done.

My tale was heard, and yet it was not told,
My fruit is fallen, and yet my leaves are green,
My youth is spent, and yet I am not old,
I saw the world, and yet I was not seen:
My thread is cut, and yet it is not spun,
And now I live, and now my life is done.

I sought my death, and found it in my womb,
I looked for life, and saw it was a shade,
I trod the earth, and knew it was my tomb,
And now I die, and now I was but made;
The glass is full, and now the glass is run,
And now I live, and now my life is done.

BATTER MY HEART, THREE-PERSON'D GOD
(1609-1611)

By John Donne

Batter my heart, three-person'd God, for you
As yet but knock, breathe, shine, and seek to mend;
That I may rise and stand, o'erthrow me, and bend
Your force to break, blow, burn, and make me new.
I, like an usurp'd town to another due,
Labor to admit you, but oh, to no end;
Reason, your viceroy in me, me should defend,
But is captiv'd, and proves weak or untrue.
Yet dearly I love you, and would be lov'd fain,
But am betroth'd unto your enemy;
Divorce me, untie or break that knot again,
Take me to you, imprison me, for I,
Except you enthrall me, never shall be free,
Nor ever chaste, except you ravish me.

THE DEFINITION OF LOVE
(1681)

By Andrew Marvell

My love is of a birth as rare
As 'tis for object strange and high;
It was begotten by Despair
Upon Impossibility.

Magnanimous Despair alone
Could show me so divine a thing
Where feeble Hope could ne'er have flown,
But vainly flapp'd its tinsel wing.

And yet I quickly might arrive
Where my extended soul is fixt,
But Fate does iron wedges drive,
And always crowds itself betwixt.

For Fate with jealous eye does see
Two perfect loves, nor lets them close;
Their union would her ruin be,
And her tyrannic pow'r depose.

And therefore her decrees of steel
Us as the distant poles have plac'd,
(Though love's whole world on us doth wheel)
Not by themselves to be embrac'd;

Unless the giddy heaven fall,
And earth some new convulsion tear;

And, us to join, the world should all
Be cramp'd into a planisphere.

As lines, so loves oblique may well
Themselves in every angle greet;
But ours so truly parallel,
Though infinite, can never meet.

Therefore the love which us doth bind,
But Fate so enviously debars,
Is the conjunction of the mind,
And opposition of the stars.

DRIFTING THROUGH THE REFLECTION OF REAL RUINS ON A LAKE CONSTRUCTED BY AN ARCHITECT
(2020)

By Laylage Courie

I am no longer pure enough to believe
in love, its archaic masquerade.
I am no longer pure enough to believe
its silken cords won't fray but
is there a love otherwise made? Of stone?
Its architecture, yes, toppled in weeds
though an entablature on slipped columns
remains to frame the inorderable sky.
I could think: It marks a grave. Or, equally:
Its austere grace! What time cracks falls away
to reveal a more essential beauty.
The ruins memorialize themselves.
Two might still walk among them hand in hand.

I KILLED A MAN
(2023)

By Laylage Courie

I killed a man.
Usually, acquiring a sickness that induces lightness,
they drift off like balloons. I wave my black handkerchief
    at the sky.
To the living, love is a plump thrush pierced by the briars
    of a flesh-pink rose.
For the dead, a flesh-feathered rose pierced by blades of
    grass drips dew.
The dead hear the bird's song in their ears because they
    have no sex organs.
It fills them with longing as for a phantom limb.
I've seen many men die.
But this man I killed.
He was beautiful and I intended to love him.
Intend, intend ...
My black handkerchief drapes the body of a broken bird.

Carlos Among the Candles
(1917)

By Wallace Stevens

THE stage is indistinguishable when the curtain rises. The room represented is semi-circular. In the center, at the back, is a large round window, covered by long curtains. There is a door at the right and one at the left. Farther forward on the stage there are two long, low, wooden tables, one at the right and one at the left. The walls and the curtains over the window are of a dark reddish-purple, with a dim pattern of antique gold.

Carlos is an eccentric pedant of about forty. He is dressed in black. He wears close-fitting breeches and a close-fitting, tightly-buttoned, short coat with long tails. His hair is rumpled. He leaps upon the stage through the door at the right. Nothing is visible through the door. He has a long thin white lighted taper, which he holds high above his head as he moves, fantastically, over the stage, examining the room in which he finds himself.

[Editor's note: To read of the lighting of candles 1-12, read the full version of Carlos Among the Candles. Here, we shall skip to the play's lyrical return to shadow.]

[When all the candles have been lighted, he runs to the center of the stage, holding his hands over his eyes. Then he returns to the window and flings aside the curtains. The light from the window falls on the tall stalks of flowers outside. The flowers are like hollyhocks, but they are unnat-

urally large, of gold and silver. He speaks excitedly.]
Where now is my solitude and the lonely figure of solitude?
Where now are the two stately ones that left their coldness
behind them? They have taken their bareness with them.
Their coldness has followed them. Here there will be silks
and fans ... the movement of arms ... rumors of Renoir ...
coiffures ... hands ... scorn of Debussy ... communications
of body to body ... There will be servants, as fat as plums,
bearing pineapples from the Azores ... because of twenty-four candles, burning together, as if their light had dispelled a phantasm, falling on silks and fans ... the movement
of arms ... The pulse of the crowd will beat out the shallow
pulses ... it will fill me.

[A strong gust of wind suddenly blows into the room,
extinguishing several of the candles on the table at the left.
He runs to the table at the left and looks, as if startled, at
the extinguished candles. He buries his head in his arms.]

That, too, was phantasm ... The night wind came into the
room ... The fans are invisible upon the floor.

[In a burst of feeling, he blows out all the candles that are
still burning on the table at the left. He crosses the stage and
stands before the table at the right. After a moment he goes
slowly to the back of the stage and draws the curtains over
the window. He returns to the table at the right.]

What is there in the extinguishing of light? It is like twelve
wild birds flying in autumn.

[He blows out one of the candles.]
It is like an eleven-limbed oak tree, brass-colored in frost

Carlos Among the Candles

... Regret ...
[He blows out another candle.]

It is like ten green sparks of a rocket, oscillating in air ...
The extinguishing of light ... how closely regret follows it.

[He blows out another candle.]

It is like the diverging angles that follow nine leaves drifting in water, and that compose themselves brilliantly on the polished surface.

[He blows out another candle.]

It is like eight pears in a nude tree, flaming in twilight ...
The extinguishing of light is like that. The season is sorrowful. The air is cold.

[He blows out another candle.]

It is like the six Pleiades, and the hidden one, that makes them seven.

[He blows out another candle.]

It is like the seven Pleiades, and the hidden one, that makes them six.

[He blows out another candle.]

The extinguishing of light is like the five purple palmations of cinquefoil withering ... It is full of the incipiences of darkness ... of desolation that rises as a feeling rises ...

Imagination wills the five purple palmations of cinquefoil.
But in this light they have the appearance of withering ...
To feel and, in the midst of feeling, to imagine ...

[He blows out another candle.]

The extinguishing of light is like the four posts of a cadaver,
two at its head and two at its feet, to-wit: its arms and legs.

[He blows out another candle.]

It is like three peregrins, departing.

[He blows out another candle.]

It is like heaven and earth in the eye of the disbeliever.

[He blows out another candle. He dances around the room.
He returns to the single candle that remains burning.]

The extinguishing of light is like that old Hesper, clapped
upon by clouds.

[He stands in front of the candle, so as to obscure it.]

The spikes of his light bristle around the edge of the bulk.
The spikes bristle among the clouds and behind them. There
is a spot where he was bright in the sky ... It remains fixed
a little in the mind.

[He opens the door at the right. Outside, the night is as
blue as water. He crosses the stage and opens the door at the
left. Once more he flings aside the curtains. He extinguishes

his taper. He looks out. He speaks with elation.]
Oh, ho! Here is matter beyond invention.

[He springs through the window.]

CURTAIN.

Eloisa to Abelard
(1717)

By Alexander Pope

In these deep solitudes and awful cells,
Where heav'nly-pensive contemplation dwells,
And ever-musing melancholy reigns;
What means this tumult in a vestal's veins?
Why rove my thoughts beyond this last retreat?
Why feels my heart its long-forgotten heat?
Yet, yet I love!—From Abelard it came,
And Eloisa yet must kiss the name.

Dear fatal name! rest ever unreveal'd,
Nor pass these lips in holy silence seal'd.
Hide it, my heart, within that close disguise,
Where mix'd with God's, his lov'd idea lies:
O write it not, my hand—the name appears
Already written—wash it out, my tears!
In vain lost Eloisa weeps and prays,
Her heart still dictates, and her hand obeys.

Relentless walls! whose darksome round contains
Repentant sighs, and voluntary pains:
Ye rugged rocks! which holy knees have worn;
Ye grots and caverns shagg'd with horrid thorn!
Shrines! where their vigils pale-ey'd virgins keep,
And pitying saints, whose statues learn to weep!
Though cold like you, unmov'd, and silent grown,
I have not yet forgot myself to stone.
All is not Heav'n's while Abelard has part,

Still rebel nature holds out half my heart;
Nor pray'rs nor fasts its stubborn pulse restrain,
Nor tears, for ages, taught to flow in vain.

Soon as thy letters trembling I unclose,
That well-known name awakens all my woes.
Oh name for ever sad! for ever dear!
Still breath'd in sighs, still usher'd with a tear.
I tremble too, where'er my own I find,
Some dire misfortune follows close behind.
Line after line my gushing eyes o'erflow,
Led through a sad variety of woe:
Now warm in love, now with'ring in thy bloom,
Lost in a convent's solitary gloom!
There stern religion quench'd th' unwilling flame,
There died the best of passions, love and fame.

Yet write, oh write me all, that I may join
Griefs to thy griefs, and echo sighs to thine.
Nor foes nor fortune take this pow'r away;
And is my Abelard less kind than they?
Tears still are mine, and those I need not spare,
Love but demands what else were shed in pray'r;
No happier task these faded eyes pursue;
To read and weep is all they now can do.

Then share thy pain, allow that sad relief;
Ah, more than share it! give me all thy grief.
Heav'n first taught letters for some wretch's aid,
Some banish'd lover, or some captive maid;
They live, they speak, they breathe what love inspires,
Warm from the soul, and faithful to its fires,
The virgin's wish without her fears impart,

Excuse the blush, and pour out all the heart,
Speed the soft intercourse from soul to soul,
And waft a sigh from Indus to the Pole.

Thou know'st how guiltless first I met thy flame,
When Love approach'd me under Friendship's name;
My fancy form'd thee of angelic kind,
Some emanation of th' all-beauteous Mind.
Those smiling eyes, attemp'ring ev'ry day,
Shone sweetly lambent with celestial day.
Guiltless I gaz'd; heav'n listen'd while you sung;
And truths divine came mended from that tongue.
From lips like those what precept fail'd to move?
Too soon they taught me 'twas no sin to love.
Back through the paths of pleasing sense I ran,
Nor wish'd an Angel whom I lov'd a Man.
Dim and remote the joys of saints I see;
Nor envy them, that heav'n I lose for thee.

How oft, when press'd to marriage, have I said,
Curse on all laws but those which love has made!
Love, free as air, at sight of human ties,
Spreads his light wings, and in a moment flies,
Let wealth, let honour, wait the wedded dame,
August her deed, and sacred be her fame;
Before true passion all those views remove,
Fame, wealth, and honour! what are you to Love?
The jealous God, when we profane his fires,
Those restless passions in revenge inspires;
And bids them make mistaken mortals groan,
Who seek in love for aught but love alone.
Should at my feet the world's great master fall,
Himself, his throne, his world, I'd scorn 'em all:

Not Caesar's empress would I deign to prove;
No, make me mistress to the man I love;
If there be yet another name more free,
More fond than mistress, make me that to thee!
Oh happy state! when souls each other draw,
When love is liberty, and nature, law:
All then is full, possessing, and possess'd,
No craving void left aching in the breast:
Ev'n thought meets thought, ere from the lips it part,
And each warm wish springs mutual from the heart.
This sure is bliss (if bliss on earth there be)
And once the lot of Abelard and me.

Alas, how chang'd! what sudden horrors rise!
A naked lover bound and bleeding lies!
Where, where was Eloise? her voice, her hand,
Her poniard, had oppos'd the dire command.
Barbarian, stay! that bloody stroke restrain;
The crime was common, common be the pain.
I can no more; by shame, by rage suppress'd,
Let tears, and burning blushes speak the rest.

Canst thou forget that sad, that solemn day,
When victims at yon altar's foot we lay?
Canst thou forget what tears that moment fell,
When, warm in youth, I bade the world farewell?
As with cold lips I kiss'd the sacred veil,
The shrines all trembl'd, and the lamps grew pale:
Heav'n scarce believ'd the conquest it survey'd,
And saints with wonder heard the vows I made.
Yet then, to those dread altars as I drew,
Not on the Cross my eyes were fix'd, but you:
Not grace, or zeal, love only was my call,

And if I lose thy love, I lose my all.
Come! with thy looks, thy words, relieve my woe;
Those still at least are left thee to bestow.
Still on that breast enamour'd let me lie,
Still drink delicious poison from thy eye,
Pant on thy lip, and to thy heart be press'd;
Give all thou canst—and let me dream the rest.
Ah no! instruct me other joys to prize,
With other beauties charm my partial eyes,
Full in my view set all the bright abode,
And make my soul quit Abelard for God.

Ah, think at least thy flock deserves thy care,
Plants of thy hand, and children of thy pray'r.
From the false world in early youth they fled,
By thee to mountains, wilds, and deserts led.
You rais'd these hallow'd walls; the desert smil'd,
And Paradise was open'd in the wild.
No weeping orphan saw his father's stores
Our shrines irradiate, or emblaze the floors;
No silver saints, by dying misers giv'n,
Here brib'd the rage of ill-requited heav'n:
But such plain roofs as piety could raise,
And only vocal with the Maker's praise.
In these lone walls (their days eternal bound)
These moss-grown domes with spiry turrets crown'd,
Where awful arches make a noonday night,
And the dim windows shed a solemn light;
Thy eyes diffus'd a reconciling ray,
And gleams of glory brighten'd all the day.
But now no face divine contentment wears,
'Tis all blank sadness, or continual tears.
See how the force of others' pray'rs I try,

(O pious fraud of am'rous charity!)
But why should I on others' pray'rs depend?
Come thou, my father, brother, husband, friend!
Ah let thy handmaid, sister, daughter move,
And all those tender names in one, thy love!
The darksome pines that o'er yon rocks reclin'd
Wave high, and murmur to the hollow wind,
The wand'ring streams that shine between the hills,
The grots that echo to the tinkling rills,
The dying gales that pant upon the trees,
The lakes that quiver to the curling breeze;
No more these scenes my meditation aid,
Or lull to rest the visionary maid.
But o'er the twilight groves and dusky caves,
Long-sounding aisles, and intermingled graves,
Black Melancholy sits, and round her throws
A death-like silence, and a dread repose:
Her gloomy presence saddens all the scene,
Shades ev'ry flow'r, and darkens ev'ry green,
Deepens the murmur of the falling floods,
And breathes a browner horror on the woods.

Yet here for ever, ever must I stay;
Sad proof how well a lover can obey!
Death, only death, can break the lasting chain;
And here, ev'n then, shall my cold dust remain,
Here all its frailties, all its flames resign,
And wait till 'tis no sin to mix with thine.

Ah wretch! believ'd the spouse of God in vain,
Confess'd within the slave of love and man.
Assist me, Heav'n! but whence arose that pray'r?
Sprung it from piety, or from despair?

Ev'n here, where frozen chastity retires,
Love finds an altar for forbidden fires.
I ought to grieve, but cannot what I ought;
I mourn the lover, not lament the fault;
I view my crime, but kindle at the view,
Repent old pleasures, and solicit new;
Now turn'd to Heav'n, I weep my past offence,
Now think of thee, and curse my innocence.
Of all affliction taught a lover yet,
'Tis sure the hardest science to forget!
How shall I lose the sin, yet keep the sense,
And love th' offender, yet detest th' offence?
How the dear object from the crime remove,
Or how distinguish penitence from love?
Unequal task! a passion to resign,
For hearts so touch'd, so pierc'd, so lost as mine.
Ere such a soul regains its peaceful state,
How often must it love, how often hate!
How often hope, despair, resent, regret,
Conceal, disdain—do all things but forget.
But let Heav'n seize it, all at once 'tis fir'd;
Not touch'd, but rapt; not waken'd, but inspir'd!
Oh come! oh teach me nature to subdue,
Renounce my love, my life, myself—and you.
Fill my fond heart with God alone, for he
Alone can rival, can succeed to thee.

How happy is the blameless vestal's lot!
The world forgetting, by the world forgot.
Eternal sunshine of the spotless mind!
Each pray'r accepted, and each wish resign'd;
Labour and rest, that equal periods keep;
"Obedient slumbers that can wake and weep;"

Desires compos'd, affections ever ev'n,
Tears that delight, and sighs that waft to Heav'n.
Grace shines around her with serenest beams,
And whisp'ring angels prompt her golden dreams.
For her th' unfading rose of Eden blooms,
And wings of seraphs shed divine perfumes,
For her the Spouse prepares the bridal ring,
For her white virgins hymeneals sing,
To sounds of heav'nly harps she dies away,
And melts in visions of eternal day.

Far other dreams my erring soul employ,
Far other raptures, of unholy joy:
When at the close of each sad, sorrowing day,
Fancy restores what vengeance snatch'd away,
Then conscience sleeps, and leaving nature free,
All my loose soul unbounded springs to thee.
Oh curs'd, dear horrors of all-conscious night!
How glowing guilt exalts the keen delight!
Provoking Daemons all restraint remove,
And stir within me every source of love.
I hear thee, view thee, gaze o'er all thy charms,
And round thy phantom glue my clasping arms.
I wake—no more I hear, no more I view,
The phantom flies me, as unkind as you.
I call aloud; it hears not what I say;
I stretch my empty arms; it glides away.
To dream once more I close my willing eyes;
Ye soft illusions, dear deceits, arise!
Alas, no more—methinks we wand'ring go
Through dreary wastes, and weep each other's woe,
Where round some mould'ring tower pale ivy creeps,
And low-brow'd rocks hang nodding o'er the deeps.

Sudden you mount, you beckon from the skies;
Clouds interpose, waves roar, and winds arise.
I shriek, start up, the same sad prospect find,
And wake to all the griefs I left behind.

For thee the fates, severely kind, ordain
A cool suspense from pleasure and from pain;
Thy life a long, dead calm of fix'd repose;
No pulse that riots, and no blood that glows.
Still as the sea, ere winds were taught to blow,
Or moving spirit bade the waters flow;
Soft as the slumbers of a saint forgiv'n,
And mild as opening gleams of promis'd heav'n.

Come, Abelard! for what hast thou to dread?
The torch of Venus burns not for the dead.
Nature stands check'd; Religion disapproves;
Ev'n thou art cold—yet Eloisa loves.
Ah hopeless, lasting flames! like those that burn
To light the dead, and warm th' unfruitful urn.

What scenes appear where'er I turn my view?
The dear ideas, where I fly, pursue,
Rise in the grove, before the altar rise,
Stain all my soul, and wanton in my eyes.
I waste the matin lamp in sighs for thee,
Thy image steals between my God and me,
Thy voice I seem in ev'ry hymn to hear,
With ev'ry bead I drop too soft a tear.
When from the censer clouds of fragrance roll,
And swelling organs lift the rising soul,
One thought of thee puts all the pomp to flight,
Priests, tapers, temples, swim before my sight:

In seas of flame my plunging soul is drown'd,
While altars blaze, and angels tremble round.

While prostrate here in humble grief I lie,
Kind, virtuous drops just gath'ring in my eye,
While praying, trembling, in the dust I roll,
And dawning grace is op'ning on my soul:
Come, if thou dar'st, all charming as thou art!
Oppose thyself to Heav'n; dispute my heart;
Come, with one glance of those deluding eyes
Blot out each bright idea of the skies;
Take back that grace, those sorrows, and those tears;
Take back my fruitless penitence and pray'rs;
Snatch me, just mounting, from the blest abode;
Assist the fiends, and tear me from my God!

No, fly me, fly me, far as pole from pole;
Rise Alps between us! and whole oceans roll!
Ah, come not, write not, think not once of me,
Nor share one pang of all I felt for thee.
Thy oaths I quit, thy memory resign;
Forget, renounce me, hate whate'er was mine.
Fair eyes, and tempting looks (which yet I view!)
Long lov'd, ador'd ideas, all adieu!
Oh Grace serene! oh virtue heav'nly fair!
Divine oblivion of low-thoughted care!
Fresh blooming hope, gay daughter of the sky!
And faith, our early immortality!
Enter, each mild, each amicable guest;
Receive, and wrap me in eternal rest!

See in her cell sad Eloisa spread,
Propp'd on some tomb, a neighbour of the dead.

In each low wind methinks a spirit calls,
And more than echoes talk along the walls.
Here, as I watch'd the dying lamps around,
From yonder shrine I heard a hollow sound.
"Come, sister, come!" (it said, or seem'd to say)
"Thy place is here, sad sister, come away!
Once like thyself, I trembled, wept, and pray'd,
Love's victim then, though now a sainted maid:
But all is calm in this eternal sleep;
Here grief forgets to groan, and love to weep,
Ev'n superstition loses ev'ry fear:
For God, not man, absolves our frailties here."

I come, I come! prepare your roseate bow'rs,
Celestial palms, and ever-blooming flow'rs.
Thither, where sinners may have rest, I go,
Where flames refin'd in breasts seraphic glow:
Thou, Abelard! the last sad office pay,
And smooth my passage to the realms of day;
See my lips tremble, and my eye-balls roll,
Suck my last breath, and catch my flying soul!
Ah no—in sacred vestments may'st thou stand,
The hallow'd taper trembling in thy hand,
Present the cross before my lifted eye,
Teach me at once, and learn of me to die.
Ah then, thy once-lov'd Eloisa see!
It will be then no crime to gaze on me.
See from my cheek the transient roses fly!
See the last sparkle languish in my eye!
Till ev'ry motion, pulse, and breath be o'er;
And ev'n my Abelard be lov'd no more.
O Death all-eloquent! you only prove
What dust we dote on, when 'tis man we love.

Then too, when fate shall thy fair frame destroy,
(That cause of all my guilt, and all my joy)
In trance ecstatic may thy pangs be drown'd,
Bright clouds descend, and angels watch thee round,
From op'ning skies may streaming glories shine,
And saints embrace thee with a love like mine.

May one kind grave unite each hapless name,
And graft my love immortal on thy fame!
Then, ages hence, when all my woes are o'er,
When this rebellious heart shall beat no more;
If ever chance two wand'ring lovers brings
To Paraclete's white walls and silver springs,
O'er the pale marble shall they join their heads,
And drink the falling tears each other sheds;
Then sadly say, with mutual pity mov'd,
"Oh may we never love as these have lov'd!"

From the full choir when loud Hosannas rise,
And swell the pomp of dreadful sacrifice,
Amid that scene if some relenting eye
Glance on the stone where our cold relics lie,
Devotion's self shall steal a thought from Heav'n,
One human tear shall drop and be forgiv'n.
And sure, if fate some future bard shall join
In sad similitude of griefs to mine,
Condemn'd whole years in absence to deplore,
And image charms he must behold no more;
Such if there be, who loves so long, so well;
Let him our sad, our tender story tell;
The well-sung woes will soothe my pensive ghost;
He best can paint 'em, who shall feel 'em most.

Abelard to Eloisa
(writ. 1720 / pub. 1728)

By Judith (Cowper) Madan

[in response to Alexander Pope's "Eloisa to Abelard"]

In my dark cell, low prostrate on the ground,
Mourning my crimes, thy Letter entrance found;
Too soon my soul the well-known name confest,
My beating heart sprang fiercely in my breast,
Thro' my whole frame a guilty transport glow'd,
And streaming torrents from my eyes fast flow'd:
 O *Eloisa*! art thou still the same?
Dost thou still nourish this destructive flame?
Have not the gentle rules of Peace and Heav'n,
From thy soft soul this fatal passion driv'n?
Alas! I thought you disengaged and free;
And can you still, still sigh and weep for me?
What powerful Deity, what hallow'd Shrine,
Can save me from a love, a faith like thine?
Where shall I fly, when not this awful Cave,
Whose rugged feet the surging billows lave;
When not these gloomy cloister's solemn walls,
O'er whose rough sides the languid ivy crawls,
When my dread vews, in vain, their force oppose?
Oppos'd to live—alas!—how vain are vows!
In fruitless penitence I wear away
Each tedious night, and sad revolving day;
I fast, I pray, and, with deceitful art,
Veil thy dear image in my tortur'd heart;
My tortur'd heart conflicting passions move.

I hope despair, repent—yet still I love:
A thousand jarring thoughts my bosom tear;
For, thou, not God, O *Eloise!* art there.
To the false world's deluding pleasures dead,
Nor longer by its wand'ring fires misled,
In learn'd disputes harsh precepts I infuse,
And give the counsel I want pow'r to use.
The rigid maxims of the grave and wife
Have quench'd each milder sparkle of my eyes:
Each lovley feature of this once lov'd face,
By grief revers'd, assumes a sterner grace;
O *Eloisa*! should the fates once more,
Indulgent to my view, thy charms restore,
How from my arms would'st thou with horror start
To miss the form familiar to thy heart;
Nought could thy quick, thy piercing judgment see,
To speak me *Abelard*—but love to thee.
Lean Abstinence, pale Grief, and haggard Care.
The dire attendants of forlorn Despair,
Have *Abelard*, the young, the gay, remov'd,
And in the Hermit funk the man you lov'd,
Wrapt in the gloom these holy mansions shed,
The thorny paths of Penitence I tread;
Lost to the world, from all its int'rests free,
And torn from all my soul held dear in thee,
Ambition with its train of frailties gone,
All loves and forms forget—but thine alone,
Amid the blaze of day, the dusk of night,
My *Eloisa* rises to my sight;
Veil'd as in Paraclete's secluded tow'rs,
The wretched mourner counts the lagging hours;
I hear her sighs, see the swift falling tears,
Weep all her griefs, and pant with all her cares.

O vows! O convent! your stern force impart,
And frown the melting phantom from my heart;
Let other sighs a worthier sorrow show,
Let other tears from sin repentance flow;
Low to the earth my guilty eyes I roll,
And humble to the dust my heaving soul,
Forgiving Pow'r! thy gracious call I meet,
Who first impower'd this rebel heart to heart;
Who thro' this trembling, this offending frame,
For nobler ends inspir'd life's active flame.
O! change the temper of this laboring breast,
And form anew each beating pulse to rest!
Let springing grace, fair faith, and hope remove
The fatal traces of destructive love!
Destructive love from his warm mansions tear,
And leave no traits of *Eloisa* there!

Are these the wishes of my inmost soul?
Would I its soft, its tend'rest sense controul?
Would I, thus touch'd, this glowing heart refine,
To the cold substance of this marble shrine?
Transform'd like these pale swarms that round me move,
Of blest insensibles—who know no love?
Ah! rather let me keep this hapless flame;
Adieu! false honour, unavailing fame!
Not your harsh rules, but tender love, supplies
The streams that gush from my despairing eyes;
I feel the traitor melt about my heart,
And thro' my veins with treacherous influence dart;
Inspire me, Heav'n! assist me, Grace divine,
Aid me, ye Saints! unknown to pains like mine;
You, who on earth serene all griefs could prove,
All but the tort'ring pangs of hopeless love;

A holier rage in your pure bosoms dwelt,
Nor can you pity what you never felt:
A sympathising grief alone can lure,
The hand that heals, must feel what I endure.
Thou, *Eloise* alone canst give me ease,
And bid my struggling soul subside to peace;
Restore me to my long lost heav'n of rest,
And take thyself from my reluctant breast;
If crimes like mine could an allay receive,
That blest allay thy wond'rons charms might give.
Thy form, that first to love my heart inclin'd,
Still wanders in my lost, my guilty mind.
I saw thee as the new blown blossoms fair,
Sprightly as light, more soft than summer's air,
Bright as their beams thy eyes a mind disclose,
Whilst on thy lips gay blush'd the fragrant rose;
Wit, youth, and love, in each dear feature shone;
Prest by my fate, I gaz'd—and was undone.
There dy'd the gen'rous fire, whose vig'rous flame
Enlarged my soul, and urg'd me on to same;
Nor fame, nor wealth, my soften'd heart could move,
Dully insensible to all but love.
Snatch'd from myself, my learning tasteless grew;
Vain my philosophy, oppos'd to you;
A train of woes succeed, nor should we mourn,
The hours that cannot, ought not to return.

As once to love I sway'd your yielding mind,
Too fond, alas! too fatally inclin'd,
To virtue now let me your breast inspire,
And fan, with zeal divine, the heav'nly fire;
Teach you to injur'd Heav'n all chang'd to turn,
And bid the soul with sacred rapture burn.

O! that my own example might impart
This noble warmth to your soft trembling heart!
That mine, with pious undissembled care,
Could aid the latent virtue struggling there;

Alas! I rave—nor grace, nor zeal divine,
Burn in a heart oppress'd with crimes like mine,
Too sure I find, while I the tortures prove
Of feeble piety, conflicting love,
On black despair my forc'd devotion's built;
Absence for me has sharper pangs than guilt.
Yet, yet, my *Eloisa*, thy charms I view,
Yet my sighs breath, my tears pour forth for you;
Each weak resistance stronger knits my chain,
I sigh, weep, love, despair, repent—in vain,
Haste, *Eloisa*, haste, your lover free,
Amidst your warmest pray'r—O think on me!
Wing with your rising zeal my grov'ling mind,
And let me mine from your repentance find!
Ah! labour, strife, your love, your self control!
The change will sure affect my kindred soul;
In blest consent our purer sighs shall breath,
And Heav'n assisting, shall our crimes forgive,
But if unhappy, wretched, lost in vain,
Faintly th' unequal combat you sustain;
If not to Heav'n you feel your bosom rise,
Nor tears refin'd fall contrite from your eyes;
If still, your heart its wonted passions move,
If still, to speak all pains in one—you love;
Deaf to the weak essays of living breath,
Attend the stronger eloquence of Death.
When that kind pow'r this captive soul shall free,
Which only then can cease to doat on thee;

When gently sunk to my eternal sleep,
The Paraclete my peaceful urn shall keep!
Then, *Eloisa*, then your lover view,
See his quench'd eyes no longer gaze on you;
From their dead orbs that tender utt'rance flown,
Which first to thine my heart's soft fate made known,
This breast no more, at length to ease consign'd,
Pant like the waving aspin in the wind;
See all my wild, tumultuous passion o'er,
And thou, amazing change! belov'd no more;
Behold the destin'd end of human love—
But let the fight your zeal alone improve;
Let not your conscious soul, to sorrow mov'd,
Recall how much, how tenderly I lov'd:
With pious care your fruitless griefs restrain,
Nor let a tear your sacred veil profane;
Not ev'n a sigh on my cold urn bestow;
But let your breast with new-born raptures glow;
Let love divine, frail mortal love dethrone,
And to your mind immortal joys make known;
Let Heav'n relenting strike your ravish'd view,
And still the bright, the blest pursuit renew!
So with your crimes shall your misfortune cease,
And your rack'd soul be calmly hush'd to peace.

LOVE ARMED
(1677)

By Aphra Behn

Song from Abdelazar

Love in Fantastic Triumph sat,
Whilst Bleeding Hearts around him flowed,
For whom Fresh pains he did Create,
And strange Tyrannic power he showed;
From thy Bright Eyes he took his fire,
Which round about, in sport he hurled;
But 'twas from mine he took desire
Enough to undo the Amorous World.

From me he took his sighs and tears,
From thee his Pride and Cruelty;
From me his Languishments and Fears,
And every Killing Dart from thee;
Thus thou and I, the God have armed,
And set him up a Deity;
But my poor Heart alone is harmed,
Whilst thine the Victor is, and free.

Verses design'd by Mrs. A. Behn to be sent to a fair Lady, that desir'd she would absent herself to cure her Love.
(1692)

By Aphra Behn

Left unfinish'd.
In vain to Woods and Deserts I retire,
To shun the lovely Charmer I admire,
Where the soft Breezes do but fann my Fire!
In vain in Grotto's dark unseen I lie,
Love pierces where the Sun could never spy.
No place, no Art his God-head can exclude,
The Dear Distemper reigns in Solitude:
Distance, alas, contributes to my Grief;
No more, of what fond Lovers call, Relief
Than to the wounded Hind does sudden Flight
From the chast Goddesses pursuing Sight:
When in the Heart the fatal Shaft remains,
And darts the Venom through our bleeding Veins.
If I resolve no longer to submit
My self a wretched Conquest to your Wit,
More swift than fleeting Shades, ten thousand Charms
From your bright Eyes that Rebel Thought disarms:
The more I strugl'd, to my Grief I found
My self in Cupid's Chains more surely bound:
Like Birds in Nets, the more I strive, I find
My self the faster in the Snare confin'd.

On the Author of that Excellent Book Intituled The Way to Health, Long Life, and Happiness.
(1682)

By Aphra Behn

Hail, Learned Bard! who dost thy power dispence,
And show'st us the first State of Innocence
In that blest golden Age, when Man was young,
When the whole Race was Vigorous and strong;
When Nature did her wond'rous dictates give,
And taught the Noble Savage how to live;
When Christal Streams, and every plenteous Wood
Afforded harmless drink, and wholsom food;
E'er that ingratitude in Man was found,
His Mother Earth with Iron Ploughs to wound;
When unconfin'd, the spacious Plains produc'd
What Nature crav'd, and more than Nature us'd;
When every Sense to innocent delight
Th' agreeing Elements unforc'd invite;
When Earth was gay, and Heaven was kind and bright,
And nothing horrid did perplex the sight;
Unprun'd the Roses and the Jes'min grew,
Nature each day drest all the World anew,
And Sweets without Mans aid each Moment grew;
Till wild Debauchery did Mens minds invade,
And Vice, and Luxury became a Trade;
Surer than War it laid whole Countrys wast,
Not Plague nor Famine ruins half so fast;
By swift degrees we took that Poison in,
Regarding not the danger, nor the sin;

ON THE AUTHOR OF THAT EXCELLENT BOOK

Delightful, Gay, and Charming was the Bait,
While Death did on th' inviting Pleasure wait,
And ev'ry Age produc'd a feebler Race,
Sickly their days, and those declin'd apace,
Scarce Blossoms Blow, and Wither in less space.
Till Nature thus declining by degrees,
We have recourse to rich restoratives,
By dull advice from some of Learned Note,
We take the Poison for the Antidote;
Till sinking Nature cloy'd with full supplys,
O'er-charg'd grows fainter, Languishes and dies.
These are the Plagues that o'er this Island reign,
And have so many threescore thousands slain;
Till you the saving Angel, whose blest hand
Have sheath'd that Sword, that threatned half the Land;
More than a Parent, Sir, we you must own,
They give but life, but you prolong it on;
You even an equal power with Heav'n do shew,
Give us long life, and lasting Vertue too:
Such were the mighty Patriarchs, of old,
Who God in all his Glory did behold,
Inspir'd like you, they Heavens Instructions show'd,
And were as Gods amidst the wandring Croud;
Not he that bore th' Almighty Wand cou'd give
Diviner Dictates, how to eat, and live.
And so essential was this cleanly Food,
For Mans eternal health, eternal good,
That God did for his first-lov'd Race provide,
What thou by Gods example hast prescrib'd:
O mai'st thou live to justify thy fame,
To Ages lasting as thy glorious Name!
May thy own life make thy vast Reasons good,
(Philosophy admir'd and understood,)

To every sense 'tis plain, 'tis great, and clear,
And Divine Wisdom does o'er all appear;
Learning and Knowledge do support the whole,
And nothing can the mighty truth controul;
Let Fools and Mad-men thy great work condemn,
I've tri'd thy Method, and adore thy Theme;
Adore the Soul that you'd such truths discern,
And scorn the fools that want the sense to learn.

Salomé (excerpts)
(1893)

By Oscar Wilde
(translated from French by Lord Alfred Douglas, 1894)[29]

[A great terrace in the Palace of Herod, set above the banqueting-hall. Some soldiers are leaning over the balcony. To the right there is a gigantic staircase, to the left, at the back, an old cistern surrounded by a wall of green bronze. Moonlight.]

The Young Syrian
How beautiful is the Princess Salomé to-night!

The Page of Herodias
Look at the moon! How strange the moon seems! She is like a woman rising from a tomb. She is like a dead woman. You would fancy she was looking for dead things.

The Young Syrian
She has a strange look. She is like a little princess who wears a yellow veil, and whose feet are of silver. She is like a princess who has little white doves for feet. You would fancy she was dancing.

The Page of Herodias
She is like a woman who is dead. She moves very slowly.

*

The Young Syrian

How pale the Princess is! Never have I seen her so pale. She is like the shadow of a white rose in a mirror of silver.

The Page of Herodias

You must not look at her. You look too much at her.

*

The Voice of Jokanaan

After me shall come another mightier than I. I am not worthy so much as to unloose the latchet of his shoes. When he cometh, the solitary places shall be glad. They shall blossom like the lily. The eyes of the blind shall see the day, and the ears of the deaf shall be opened. The new-born child shall put his hand upon the dragon's lair, he shall lead the lions by their manes.

Second Soldier

Make him be silent, He is always saying ridiculous things.

First Soldier

No, no. He is a holy man. He is very gentle, too. Every day when I give him to eat he thanks me.

The Cappadocian

Who is he?

First Soldier

A prophet.

The Cappadocian

What is his name ?

First Soldier
Jokanaan.

*

The Young Syrian
The Princess has hidden her face behind her fan! Her little white hands are fluttering like doves that fly to their dove-cots. They are like white butterflies. They are just like white butterflies.

The Page of Herodias
What is that to you? Why do you look at her? You must not look at her ... Something terrible may happen.

*

The Young Syrian
The Princess rises! She is leaving the table! She looks very troubled. Ah, she is coming this way. Yes, she is coming towards us. How pale she is! Never have I seen her so pale.

The Page of Herodias
Do not look at her. I pray you not to look at her.

The Young Syrian
She is like a dove that has strayed ... She is like a narcissus trembling in the wind ... She is like a silver flower.

[Enter Salomé.]

Salomé
I will not stay. I cannot stay. Why does the Tetrarch look at

me all the while with his mole's eyes under his shaking eyelids? It is strange that the husband of my mother looks at me like that. I know not what it means. In truth, yes, I know it.

*

Salomé

How good to see the moon! She is like a little piece of money. You would think she was a little silver flower. The moon is cold and chaste. I am sure she is a virgin, she has a virgin's beauty. Yes, she is a virgin. She has never defiled herself. She has never abandoned herself to men, like the other goddesses.

The Voice of Jokanaan

The Lord hath come. The Son of Man hath come. The centaurs have hidden themselves in the rivers, and the sirens have left the rivers, and are lying beneath the leaves in the forests.

Salomé

Who was that who cried out?

Second Soldier

The prophet, Princess.

*

Salomé

I desire to speak with him.

First Soldier

It is impossible, Princess.

Salomé
I will speak with him.

The Young Syrian
Would it not be better to return to the banquet?

Salomé
Bring forth this prophet.

*

The Page of Herodias
Oh! How strange the moon looks. You would think it was the hand of a dead woman who is seeking to cover herself with a shroud.

The Young Syrian
The moon has a strange look! She is like a little princess, whose eyes are eyes of amber. Through the clouds of muslin she is smiling like a little princess.

[The prophet comes out of the cistern. Salomé looks at him and steps slowly back.]

*

Salomé
It is his eyes above all that are terrible. They are like black holes burned by torches in a Tyrian tapestry. They are like black caverns where dragons dwell. They are like the black caverns of Egypt in which the dragons make their lairs. They are like black lakes troubled by fantastic moons ... Do you think he will speak again?

THE YOUNG SYRIAN
Do not stay here, Princess. I pray you do not stay here.

SALOMÉ
How wasted he is! He is like a thin ivory statue. He is like an image of silver. I am sure he is chaste as the moon is. He is like a moonbeam, like a shaft of silver. His flesh must be cool like ivory. I would look closer at him.

THE YOUNG SYRIAN
No, no, Princess.

SALOMÉ
I must look at him closer.

THE YOUNG SYRIAN
Princess! Princess!

JOKANAAN
Who is this woman who is looking at me? I will not have her look at me. Wherefore doth she look at me with her golden eyes, under her gilded eyelids? I know not who she is. I do not wish to know who she is. Bid her begone. It is not to her that I would speak.

SALOMÉ
I am Salomé, daughter of Herodias, Princess of Judæa.

JOKANAAN
Back! daughter of Babylon! Come not near the chosen of the Lord. Thy mother hath filled the earth with the wine of her iniquities, and the cry of her sins hath come up to the ears of God.

Salomé
Speak again, Jokanaan. Thy voice is wine to me.

The Young Syrian
Princess! Princess! Princess!

Salomé
Speak again! Speak again, Jokanaan, and tell me what I must do.

Jokanaan
Daughter of Sodom, come not near me! But cover thy face with a veil, and scatter ashes upon thine head, and get thee to the desert and seek out the Son of Man.

Salomé
Who is he, the Son of Man? Is he as beautiful as thou art, Jokanaan?

Jokanaan
Get thee behind me! I hear in the palace the beating of the wings of the angel of death.

*

Salomé
Jokanaan!

Jokanaan
Who speaketh?

Salomé
Jokanaan, I am amorous of thy body! Thy body is white

like the lilies of a field that the mower hath never mowed. Thy body is white like the snows that lie on the mountains, like the snows that lie on the mountains of Judæa, and come down into the valleys. The roses in the garden of the Queen of Arabia are not so white as thy body. Neither the roses in the garden of the Queen of Arabia, the perfumed garden of spices of the Queen of Arabia, nor the feet of the dawn when they light on the leaves, nor the breast of the moon when she lies on the breast of the sea ... There is nothing in the world so white as thy body. Let me touch thy body.

Jokanaan

Back! daughter of Babylon! By woman came evil into the world. Speak not to me. I will not listen to thee. I listen but to the voice of the Lord God.

Salomé

Thy body is hideous. It is like the body of a leper. It is like a plastered wall where vipers have crawled; like a plastered wall where the scorpions have made their nest. It is like a whitened sepulchre full of loathsome things. It is horrible, thy body is horrible. It is of thy hair that I am enamoured, Jokanaan. Thy hair is like clusters of grapes, like the clusters of black grapes that hang from the vine-trees of Edom in the land of the Edomites. Thy hair is like the cedars of Lebanon, like the great cedars of Lebanon that give their shade to the lions and to the robbers who would hide themselves by day. The long black nights, when the moon hides her face, when the stars are afraid, are not so black. The silence that dwells in the forest is not so black. There is nothing in the world so black as thy hair ... Let me touch thy hair.

JOKANAAN
Back, daughter of Sodom! Touch me not. Profane not the temple of the Lord God.

SALOMÉ
Thy hair is horrible. It is covered with mire and dust. It is like a crown of thorns which they have placed on thy forehead. It is like a knot of black serpents writhing round thy neck. I love not thy hair ... It is thy mouth that I desire, Jokanaan. Thy mouth is like a band of scarlet on a tower of ivory. It is like a pomegranate cut with a knife of ivory. The pomegranate-flowers that blossom in the gardens of Tyre, and are redder than roses, are not so red. The red blasts of trumpets that herald the approach of kings, and make afraid the enemy, are not so red. Thy mouth is redder than the feet of those who tread the wine in the wine-press. Thy mouth is redder than the feet of the doves who haunt the temples and are fed by the priests. It is redder than the feet of him who cometh from a forest where he hath slain a lion, and seen gilded tigers. Thy mouth is like a branch of coral that fishers have found in the twilight of the sea, the coral that they keep for the kings! ... It is like the vermilion that the Moabites find in the mines of Moab, the vermilion that the kings take from them. It is like the bow of the King of the Persians, that is painted with vermilion, and is tipped with coral. There is nothing in the world so red as thy mouth ... Let me kiss thy mouth.

JOKANAAN
Never! daughter of Babylon! Daughter of Sodom! Never.

SALOMÉ
I will kiss thy mouth, Jokanaan. I will kiss thy mouth.

The Young Syrian

Princess, Princess, thou who art like a garden of myrrh, thou who art the dove of all doves, look not at this man, look not at him! Do not speak such words to him. I cannot suffer them ... Princess, Princess, do not speak these things.

Salomé

I will kiss thy mouth, Jokanaan.

The Young Syrian

Ah! [He kills himself and falls between Salomé and Jokanaan.]

*

Salomé

Let me kiss thy mouth.

Jokanaan

Cursed be thou! daughter of an incestuous mother, be thou accursed!

Salomé

I will kiss thy mouth, Jokanaan.

Jokanaan

I do no wish to look at thee. I will not look at thee, thou art accursed, Salomé, thou art accursed. [He goes down into the cistern.]

Salomé

I will kiss thy mouth, Jokanaan; I will kiss thy mouth.

*

HERODIAS
You must not look at her! You are always looking at her!

HEROD
The moon has a strange look to-night. Has she not a strange look? She is like a mad woman, a mad woman who is seeking everywhere for lovers. She is naked too. She is quite naked. The clouds are seeking to clothe her nakedness, but she will not let them. She shows herself naked in the sky. She reels through the clouds like a drunken woman ... I am sure she is looking for lovers. Does she not reel like a drunken woman? She is like a mad woman, is she not?

*

HEROD
By my life, by my crown, by my gods. Whatsoever you desire I will give it you, even to the half of my kingdom, if you will but dance for me. O, Salomé, Salomé, dance for me!

SALOMÉ
You have sworn, Tetrarch.

HEROD
I have sworn, Salomé.

SALOMÉ
All this I ask, even the half of your kingdom.

HERODIAS

My daughter, do not dance.

HEROD

Even to the half of my kingdom. Thou wilt be passing fair as a queen, Salomé, if it please thee to ask for the half of my kingdom. Will she not be fair as a queen? Ah! it is cold here! There is an icy wind, and I hear ... wherefore do I hear in the air this beating of wings? Ah! one might fancy a bird, a huge black bird that hovers over the terrace. Why can I not see it, this bird? The beat of its wings is terrible. The breath of the wind of its wings is terrible. It is a chill wind. Nay, but it is not cold, it is hot. I am choking. Pour water on my hands. Give me snow to eat. Loosen my mantle. Quick! quick! loosen my mantle. Nay, but leave it. It is my garland that hurts me, my garland of roses. The flowers are like fire. They have burned my forehead. [He tears the wreath from his head and throws it on the table.] Ah! I can breathe now. How red those petals are! They are like stains of blood on the cloth. That does not matter. You must not find symbols in everything you see. It makes life impossible. It were better to say that stains of blood are as lovely as rose petals. It were better far to say that ... But we will not speak of this. Now I am happy, I am passing happy. Have I not the right to be happy? Your daughter is going to dance for me. Will you not dance for me, Salomé? You have promised to dance for me.

HERODIAS

I will not have her dance.

*

HEROD
Ah, you are going to dance with naked feet. 'Tis well!—'Tis well. Your little feet will be like white doves. They will be like little white flowers that dance upon the trees ... No, no, she is going to dance on blood. There is blood spilt on the ground. She must not dance on blood. It were an evil omen.

HERODIAS
What is it to you if she dance on blood? Thou hast waded deep enough therein ...

HEROD
What is it to me? Ah! look at the moon! She has become red. She has become red as blood. Ah! the prophet prophesied truly. He prophesied that the moon would become red as blood. Did he not prophesy it? All of you heard him. And now the moon has become red as blood. Do ye not see it?

HERODIAS
Oh, yes, I see it well, and the stars are falling like ripe figs, are they not? and the sun is becoming black like sackcloth of hair, and the kings of the earth are afraid. That at least one can see. The prophet, for once in his life, was right, the kings of the earth are afraid ... Let us go within. You are sick. They will say at Rome that you are mad. Let us go within, I tell you.

*

[Salomé dances the dance of the seven veils.]

*

Salomé

[Kneeling] I would that they presently bring me in a silver charger ...

Herod

[Laughing] In a silver charger? Surely yes, in a silver charger. She is charming, is she not? What is it you would have in a silver charger, O sweet and fair Salomé, you who are fairer than all the daughters of Judæa? What would you have them bring thee in a silver charger? Tell me. Whatsoever it may be, they shall give it you. My treasures belong to thee. What is it, Salomé?

Salomé

[Rising] The head of Jokanaan.

Herodias

Ah! that is well said, my daughter.

Herod

No, no!

Herodias

That is well said, my daughter.

Herod

No, no, Salomé. You do not ask me that. Do not listen to your mother's voice. She is ever giving you evil counsel. Do not heed her.

Salomé

I do not heed my mother. It is for mine own pleasure that I ask the head of Jokanaan in a silver charger. You hath sworn, Herod. Forget not that you have sworn an oath.

HEROD
I know it. I have sworn by my gods. I know it well. But I pray you, Salomé, ask of me something else. Ask of me the half of my kingdom, and I will give it you. But ask not of me what you have asked.

SALOMÉ
I ask of you the head of Jokanaan.

*

HEROD
Be silent, speak not to me! ... Come, Salomé, be reasonable. I have never been hard to you. I have ever loved you ... It may be that I have loved you too much. Therefore ask not this thing of me. This is a terrible thing, an awful thing to ask of me. Surely, I think thou art jesting. The head of a man that is cut from his body is ill to look upon, is it not? It is not meet that the eyes of a virgin should look upon such a thing. What pleasure could you have in it? None. No, no, it is not what you desire. Hearken to me. I have an emerald, a great round emerald, which Cæsar's minion sent me. If you look through this emerald you can see things which happen at a great distance. Cæsar himself carries such an emerald when he goes to the circus. But my emerald is larger. I know well that it is larger. It is the largest emerald in the whole world. You would like that, would you not? Ask it of me and I will give it you.

SALOMÉ
I demand the head of Jokanaan.

HEROD

You are not listening. You are not listening. Suffer me to speak, Salomé.

SALOMÉ

The head of Jokanaan.

HEROD

No, no, you would not have that. You say that to trouble me, because I have looked at you all this evening. It is true, I have looked at you all this evening. Your beauty troubled me. Your beauty has grievously troubled me, and I have looked at you too much. But I will look at you no more. Neither at things, nor at people should one look. Only in mirrors should one look, for mirrors do but show us masks. Oh! oh! bring wine! I thirst ... Salomé, Salomé, let us be friends. Come now! ... Ah! what would I say? What was't? Ah! I remember! ... Salomé—nay, but come nearer to me; I fear you will not hear me—Salomé, you know my white peacocks, my beautiful white peacocks, that walk in the garden between the myrtles and the tall cypress trees. Their beaks are gilded with gold, and the grains that they eat are gilded with gold also, and their feet are stained with purple. When they cry out the rain comes, and the moon shows herself in the heavens when they spread their tails. Two by two they walk between the cypress trees and the black myrtles, and each has a slave to tend it. Sometimes they fly across the trees, and anon they crouch in the grass, and round the lake. There are not in all the world birds so wonderful. There is no king in all the world who possesses such wonderful birds. I am sure that Cæsar himself has no birds so fair as my birds. I will give you fifty of my peacocks. They will follow you whithersoever you go, and in the midst of them you will be

like the moon in the midst of a great white cloud ... I will
give them all to you. I have but a hundred, and in the whole
world there is no king who has peacocks like unto my peacocks. But I will give them all to you. Only you must loose
me from my oath, and must not ask of me that which you
have asked of me. [He empties the cup of wine.]

Salomé
Give me the head of Jokanaan.

Herodias
Well said, my daughter! As for you, you are ridiculous with
your peacocks.

Herod
Be silent! You cry out always; you cry out like a beast of
prey. You must not. Your voice wearies me. Be silent, I
say Salomé, think of what you are doing. This man comes
perchance from God. He is a holy man. The finger of God
has touched him. God has put into his mouth terrible words.
In the palace as in the desert God is always with him ... At
least it is possible. One does not know. It is possible that
God is for him and with him. Furthermore, if he died some
misfortune might happen to me. In any case, he said that
the day he dies a misfortune will happen to some one. That
could only be to me. Remember, I slipped in blood when I
entered. Also, I heard a beating of wings in the air, a beating
of mighty wings. These are very evil omens, and there were
others. I am sure there were others though I did not see
them. Well, Salomé, you do not wish a misfortune to happen
to me? You do not wish that. Listen to me, then.

Salomé

Give me the head of Jokanaan.

Herod

Ah! you are not listening to me. Be calm. I—I am calm. I am quite calm. Listen. I have jewels hidden in this place— jewels that your mother even has never seen; jewels that are marvellous. I have a collar of pearls, set in four rows. They are like unto moons chained with rays of silver. They are like fifty moons caught in a golden net. On the ivory of her breast a queen has worn it. Thou shalt be as fair as a queen when thou wearest it. I have amethysts of two kinds, one that is black like wine, and one that is red like wine which has been coloured with water. I have topazes, yellow as are the eyes of tigers, and topazes that are pink as the eyes of a wood-pigeon, and green topazes that are as the eyes of cats. I have opals that burn always, with an icelike flame, opals that make sad men's minds, and are fearful of the shadows. I have onyxes like the eyeballs of a dead woman. I have moonstones that change when the moon changes, and are wan when they see the sun. I have sapphires big like eggs, and as blue as blue flowers. The sea wanders within them and the moon comes never to trouble the blue of their waves. I have chrysolites and beryls and chrysoprases and rubies. I have sardonyx and hyacinth stones, and stones of chalcedony, and I will give them all to you, all, and other things will I add to them. The King of the Indies has but even now sent me four fans fashioned from the feathers of parrots, and the King of Numidia a garment of ostrich feathers. I have a crystal, into which it is not lawful for a woman to look, nor may young men behold it until they have been beaten with rods. In a coffer of nacre I have three wondrous turquoises. He who wears them on his forehead can imagine things which are not, and he who carries them in his hand can make women sterile. These are great treasures above all price. They are treasures without price. But this is not all. In an ebony coffer I have two cups of amber, that are like apples of gold. If an enemy pour poison into these cups, they become like an apple of silver. In a coffer incrusted with amber I have sandals incrusted with glass. I have mantles that have been brought from the land of the Seres, and bracelets decked about with carbuncles and with jade that come from the city of Euphrates ... What desirest thou more than this, Salomé? Tell me the thing that thou desirest, and I will give it thee. All that thou askest I will give thee, save one thing. I will give thee all that is mine, save one life. I will give thee the mantle of the high priest. I will give thee the veil of the sanctuary.

The Jews
Oh! oh!

Salomé
Give me the head of Jokanaan.

Herod
[Sinking back in his seat] Let her be given what she asks! Of a truth she is her mother's child!

*

Salomé
[She leans over the cistern and listens.] There is no sound. I hear nothing. Why does he not cry out, this man? Ah! if any man sought to kill me, I would cry out, I would struggle, I would not suffer ... Strike, strike, Naaman, strike, I tell

you ... No, I hear nothing. There is a silence, a terrible silence. Ah! something has fallen upon the ground. I heard something fall. It is the sword of the headsman. He is afraid, this slave. He has let his sword fall. He dare not kill him. He is a coward, this slave! Let soldiers be sent. [She sees the Page of Herodias and addresses him.] Come hither, thou wert the friend of him who is dead, is it not so? Well, I tell thee, there are not dead men enough. Go to the soldiers and bid them go down and bring me the thing I ask, the thing the Tetrarch has promised me, the thing that is mine. [The Page recoils. She turns to the soldiers.] Hither, ye soldiers. Get ye down into this cistern and bring me the head of this man. [The Soldiers recoil.] Tetrarch, Tetrarch, command your soldiers that they bring me the head of Jokanaan.

[A huge black arm, the arm of the Executioner, comes forth from the cistern, bearing on a silver shield the head of Jokanaan. Salomé seizes it. Herod hides his face with his cloak. Herodias smiles and fans herself. The Nazarenes fall on their knees and begin to pray.]

Ah! thou wouldst not suffer me to kiss thy mouth, Jokanaan. Well! I will kiss it now. I will bite it with my teeth as one bites a ripe fruit. Yes, I will kiss thy mouth, Jokanaan. I said it; did I not say it? I said it. Ah! I will kiss it now ... But, wherefore dost thou not look at me, Jokanaan? Thine eyes that were so terrible, so full of rage and scorn, are shut now. Wherefore are they shut? Open thine eyes! Lift up thine eyelids, Jokanaan! Wherefore dost thou not look at me? Art thou afraid of me, Jokanaan, that thou wilt not look at me? ... And thy tongue, that was like a red snake darting poison, it moves no more, it says nothing now, Jokanaan, that scarlet viper that spat its venom upon me. It is strange, is it not? How is it that the red viper stirs no longer? ... Thou wouldst have none of me, Jokanaan. Thou didst reject me. Thou didst speak evil words against me. Thou didst treat me as a harlot, as a wanton, me, Salomé, daughter of Herodias, Princess of Judæa! Well, Jokanaan, I still live, but thou, thou art dead, and thy head belongs to me. I can do with it what I will. I can throw it to the dogs and to the birds of the air. That which the dogs leave, the birds of the air shall devour ... Ah, Jokanaan, Jokanaan, thou wert the only man that I have loved. All other men are hateful to me. But thou, thou wert beautiful! Thy body was a column of ivory set on a silver socket. It was a garden full of doves and of silver lilies. It was a tower of silver decked with shields of ivory. There was nothing in the world so white as thy body. There was nothing in the world so black as thy hair. In the whole world there was nothing so red as thy mouth. Thy voice was a censer that scattered strange perfumes, and when I looked on thee I heard a strange music. Ah! wherefore didst thou not look at me, Jokanaan? Behind thine hands and thy curses thou didst hide thy face. Thou didst put upon thine eyes the covering of him who would see his God. Well, thou hast seen thy God, Jokanaan, but me, me, thou didst never see. If thou hadst seen me thou wouldst have loved me. I, I saw thee, Jokanaan, and I loved thee. Oh, how I loved thee! I love thee yet, Jokanaan, I love thee only ... I am athirst for thy beauty; I am hungry for thy body; and neither wine nor fruits can appease my desire. What shall I do now, Jokanaan? Neither the floods nor the great waters can quench my passion. I was a princess, and thou didst scorn me. I was a virgin, and thou didst take my virginity from me. I was chaste, and thou didst fill my veins with fire ... Ah! ah! wherefore didst thou not look at me, Jokanaan? If thou hadst looked at me thou hadst loved me. Well I know that thou wouldst have loved me, and the mystery of love is greater than the mystery of death. Love only should one consider.

*

[The slaves put out the torches. The stars disappear. A great black cloud crosses the moon and conceals it completely. The stage becomes very dark. The Tetrarch begins to climb the staircase.]

THE VOICE OF SALOMÉ

Ah! I have kissed thy mouth, Jokanaan, I have kissed thy mouth. There was a bitter taste on thy lips. Was it the taste of blood? ... But perchance it is the taste of love ... They say that love hath a bitter taste .... But what of that? what of that? I have kissed thy mouth, Jokanaan.

[A moonbeam falls on Salomé covering her with light.]

HEROD

[Turning round and seeing Salomé.] Kill that woman!

[The soldiers rush forward and crush beneath their shields Salomé, daughter of Herodias, Princess of Judæa.]

CURTAIN.

The Body of the Father Christian Rosencrux
(1895)

By William Butler Yeats

The followers of the Father Christian Rosencrux, says the old tradition, wrapped his imperishable body in noble raiment and laid it under the house of their order, in a tomb containing the symbols of all things in heaven and earth, and in the waters under the earth, and set about him inextinguishable magical lamps, which burnt on generation after generation, until other students of the order came upon the tomb by chance. It seems to me that the imagination has had no very different history during the last two hundred years, but has been laid in a great tomb of criticism, and had set over it inextinguishable magical lamps of wisdom and romance, and has been altogether so nobly housed and apparelled that we have forgotten that its wizard lips are closed, or but opened for the complaining of some melancholy and ghostly voice. The ancients and the Elizabethans abandoned themselves to imagination as a woman abandons herself to love, and created great beings who made the people of this world seem but shadows, and great passions which made our loves and hatreds appear but ephemeral and trivial phantasies; but now it is not the great persons, or the great passions we imagine, which absorb us, for the persons and passions in our poems are mainly reflections our mirror has caught from older poems or from the life about us, but the wise comments we make upon them, the criticism of life we wring from their fortunes. Arthur and his Court are nothing, but the many-coloured lights that play about them are as beautiful as the lights from cathedral windows; Pompilia and Guido are but little, while the ever-recurring meditations and expositions which climax in the mouth of the Pope are among the wisest of the Christian age. I cannot get it out of my mind that this age of criticism is about to pass, and an age of imagination, of emotion, of moods, of revelation, about to come in its place; for certainly belief in a supersensual world is at hand again; and when the notion that we are 'phantoms of the earth and water' has gone down the wind, we will trust our own being and all it desires to invent; and when the external world is no more the standard of reality, we will learn again that the great Passions are angels of God, and that to embody them 'uncurbed in their eternal glory,' even in their labour for the ending of man's peace and prosperity, is more than to comment, however wisely, upon the tendencies of our time, or to express the socialistic, or humanitarian, or other forces of our time, or even 'to sum up' our time, as the phrase is; for Art is a revelation, and not a criticism, and the life of the artist is in the old saying, 'The wind bloweth where it listeth, and thou hearest the sound thereof, but canst not tell whence it cometh and whither it goeth; so is every one that is born of the spirit.'

William Blake and the Imagination
(1897)

By William Butler Yeats

There have been men who loved the future like a mistress, and the future mixed her breath into their breath and shook her hair about them, and hid them from the understanding of their times. William Blake was one of these men, and if he spoke confusedly and obscurely it was because he spoke of things for whose speaking he could find no models in the world about him. He announced the religion of art, of which no man dreamed in the world about him; and he understood it more perfectly than the thousands of subtle spirits who have received its baptism in the world about us, because, in the beginning of important things—in the beginning of love, in the beginning of the day, in the beginning of any work, there is a moment when we understand more perfectly than we understand again until all is finished. In his time educated people believed that they amused themselves with books of imagination, but that they 'made their souls' by listening to sermons and by doing or by not doing certain things. When they had to explain why serious people like themselves honoured the great poets greatly they were hard put to it for lack of good reasons. In our time we are agreed that we 'make our souls' out of some one of the great poets of ancient times, or out of Shelley or Wordsworth, or Goethe or Balzac, or Flaubert, or Count Tolstoy, in the books he wrote before he became a prophet and fell into a lesser order, or out of Mr. Whistler's pictures, while we amuse ourselves, or, at best, make a poorer sort of soul, by listening to sermons or by doing or by not doing certain things. We write of great writers, even of writers whose beauty would once have seemed an unholy beauty, with rapt sentences like those our fathers kept for the beatitudes and mysteries of the Church; and no matter what we believe with our lips, we believe with our hearts that beautiful things, as Browning said in his one prose essay that was not in verse, have 'lain burningly on the Divine hand,' and that when time has begun to wither, the Divine hand will fall heavily on bad taste and vulgarity. When no man believed these things William Blake believed them, and began that preaching against the Philistine, which is as the preaching of the Middle Ages against the Saracen.

He had learned from Jacob Boehme and from old alchemist writers that imagination was the first emanation of divinity, 'the body of God,' 'the Divine members,' and he drew the deduction, which they did not draw, that the imaginative arts were therefore the greatest of Divine revelations, and that the sympathy with all living things, sinful and righteous alike, which the imaginative arts awaken, is that forgiveness of sins commanded by Christ. The reason, and by the reason he meant deductions from the observations of the senses, binds us to mortality because it binds us to the senses, and divides us from each other by showing us our clashing interests; but imagination divides us from mortality by the immortality of beauty, and binds us to each other by opening the secret doors of all hearts. He cried again and again that every thing that lives is holy, and that nothing is unholy except things that do not live—lethargies, and cruelties, and timidities, and that denial of imagination which is the root they grew from in old times. Passions, because most living, are most holy—and this was a scandalous paradox in his time—and man shall enter eternity borne upon their wings

Endnotes

Unless otherwise noted, quotes derive from Betty Radice's translation of *The Letters of Abelard & Heloise* (Penguin Classic Edition, 2004; revised by Michael Clanchy).

1   'Do not play the lion in your house, upsetting your household ... '

2   'I cannot be equally with men and God.'

3   'I have slipped off my dress: must I put it on again?'

4   'Night after night on my bed I have sought my true love.'

5   So indeed the true sun changes her colour because the heavenly love of the bridegroom humbles her like this, or torments her with tribulations ...

6   ... the importance of the problem was matched by the subtlety of my solution

7   'From the end of the earth I have called to thee when my heart was in anguish'

8   The more we possess which can be lost, the greater the fear which torments us ...

9   'The tongue is a small member of the body, but how great a fire! How vast a forest it can set alight!'

10   'Do not look at the wine when it glows and sparkles in the glass.'

11   This woman in face, disdained or feared to rise from the bed of her contemplation.

12   I ... propose to instruct your way of life through the many documents of the holy Fathers ... gathering each blossom as it comes to mind and collecting in a single bunch what I shall ...

13   'Whoever sits in solitude and is at peace is rescued from three wars ...; he shall have only one thing to fight against, the heart.'

14   And, although we may be enclosed in cloisters in the body, the mind still loves things outside, has an urge to pursue them ...

15   'Always we seek the forbidden and desire what is denied.'

16   Such a wife desires private, not public delights with her husband, and would rather be experienced in bed that seen at table.

17   ... all his miracles were performed either in lonely or hidden places.

18   I embrace in the arms of faith him who acts divinely in the glorious flesh of a virgin which he assumed from the Paraclete.

19   'Do you not know that your body is a shrine of the in-dwelling Holy Spirit ... '

20   'This is not offering a kiss but proffering a cup.'

21   What more?

22   ... logic has made me hated by the world.

23   The storm may rage but I am unshaken, though the winds may blow they leave me unmoved; for the rock of my foundation stands firm.

24   extracted from Abelard's treatise *Sic et Non* as translated on the public domain bibliofile site

25 And so I took myself off to a lonely spot I had known before ... 'Lo, I excaped far away and found a refuge in the wilderness.'

26 My love, which brought us both to sin, should be called lust, not love. I took my fill of my wretched pleasures in you, and this was the sum total of my love.

27 An equal to an equal, to a reddening rose under the spotless whiteness of lilies: whatever a lover gives to a lover.

28 Indeed your words are few, but I made them many by re-reading them often.

29 Excerpts of *Salomé* are adapted from the Project Gutenberg public domain text (pub. May 12, 2013).

The Author

Laylage Courie is a writer and performer who makes things from words; things includes concept albums, art-pop songs, collage, performances, poems, and genre-bending texts such as *Intimate Things.*

Her work has appeared on stages all over New York, streaming through sound systems all over the world, and in literary publications including *Fence, Adbusters,* and the performance journal *The Open Page.* She lives on the vertices of the triangle between Georgia, New York City, and the Delaware River Valley, with the enchantments of her imagination and a potted garden for companions. Her recording of Heloise's Song is available online for your listening pleasure; you can find it and much more at luminouswork.org.

Notes

Page Number	Musings & Reflections

www.ingramcontent.com/pod-product-compliance
Lightning Source LLC
Chambersburg PA
CBHW030442010526
44118CB00011B/751